THE DISABLED
DISCIPLE

THE DISABLED DISCIPLE

Ministering In A Church *Without* Barriers

ELIZABETH J. BROWNE, PH.D.

LIGUORI
PUBLICATIONS

One Liguori Drive
Liguori, MO 63057-9999
(314) 464-2500

Imprimi Potest:
Richard Thibodeau, C.SS.R.
Provincial, Denver Province
The Redemptorists

Imprimatur:
+ Paul A. Zipfel, V.G.
Auxiliary Bishop, Archdiocese of St. Louis

ISBN 0-7648-0045-0

Library of Congress Catalog Card Number: 96-78936

Scripture quotations are taken from the *New Revised Standard Version
Bible,* copyright © 1989 by the Division of Christian Education of the
National Council of the Churches of Christ in the U.S.A. Used by
permission. All rights reserved.

Excerpts from *Celebrate and Challenge: On the Ten Year Anniversary
of the Pastoral Statement on Persons with Disabilities* © 1988; *Guidelines
for the Celebration of the Sacraments with Persons with Disabilities* ©
1995; *Pastoral Letter on the Economy* © 1986; *Pastoral Statement of
U.S. Catholic Bishops on Persons with Disabilities* © 1978, United States
Catholic Conference, Washington, D.C., are used with permission. All
rights reserved.

"For the Time Being" from W. H. AUDEN: COLLECTED POEMS by
W. H. Auden, edited by Edward Mendelson. Copyright © 1944 and
renewed 1972 by W. H. Auden. Reprinted by permission of Random
House, Inc.

Printed in the United States of America
01 00 99 98 97 5 4 3 2 1
First Edition
Cover design by Christine Kraus
Cover photo by W. P. Wittman

Blessed Woman,

Excellent Man,

Redeem for the dull the

Average Way,

That common ungifted

Natures may

Believe that their normal

Vision can

Walk to perfection.

W. H. Auden

CONTENTS

FOREWORD

The author of this enticing and powerful book has not only composed its message but embodied its truth. For many years and to countless people she has proclaimed the gospel through her tenacious commitment to justice and inclusion.

The Disabled Disciple represents the kind of theology that has brought new vitality to the Church in the wake of the Second Vatican Council. It is a theology that refuses to be abstract or insulated from people's lives. This work draws its theological vision and its pastoral wisdom not only from the wellsprings of the Scriptures and the Church's teaching but also from profound Christian experience. It is theology from the ground up. And in the spirit of Jesus who had extraordinary rapport with those pushed to the margins, the message of *The Disabled Disciple* brings into play the experiences of those who have disabilities. The experiences of those who seek God and live our their baptismal commitment while sometimes experiencing exclusion, isolation, or—even worse—patronizing treatment from others in the Christian community form a unique vantage point that the entire Church needs to hear.

Anyone who knows Elizabeth Browne is aware of her strong faith and her boundless determination (along with equal doses of good humor and graciousness). I am reminded of many of the characters in the gospel stories she cites in this book: the Canaanite woman who stops Jesus in his tracks on behalf of her seriously ill daughter; the woman with the hemorrhage who pushes through the crowd to touch Jesus' cloak; the woman bent double who stands up straight and begins to shout praises to God; Bartimaeus who shouts out Jesus' name over the protests of the disciples; and, of course, the man born blind who exults in his liberating encounter with Jesus while the religious leaders fume. The gospel cites the "faith" of each of these characters—"faith" not simply in the sense that they understood the power of Jesus, but the kind of faith that made them determined to seek full life despite the obstacles.

This is the kind of active, determined, and practical faith on display in this book. Pastoral staffs, those with disabilities (along with their families and friends), caregivers, and just any thoughtful Christian will be enriched, instructed, and even inspired.

DONALD SENIOR, C.P.
CATHOLIC THEOLOGICAL UNION

PREFACE

Ministries involved with and dedicated to persons with disabilities are increasing in many churches. They are offering promise and hope for countless persons who have too long been overlooked, ignored, and discounted as unworthy of serious attention. That is dramatically changing, fortunately, and it is our purpose in this book

- First, to explore how and why the Church established by the Holy Spirit has always been concerned for the poor, the disabled, and the marginalized.
- Second, to identify modern society's outcasts and understand their need for the Church's ministering touch.
- Third, to recognize that persons with disabilities can contribute to these ministries.
- Fourth, to realize that goodwill is not enough, and that sensitivity, education, and training are essential components of successful ministries.
- And finally, to show how, through these efforts, we may begin to discern the kingdom of God in our very midst.

Our faith proudly asserts, and all Christians believe, that the crucified Jesus Christ is the central symbol of our faith—

the Crucified One, our disabled God, our paradigm. This is our faith.

Yet when we call our God disabled, we pause, we are shocked, we find this restating of our basic beliefs to be almost blasphemous. Perhaps this is because we so casually accept the crucifixion that by casting it in different words we have to confront what Christ crucified actually means.

Jesus was the Word Incarnate. While remaining fully God, he took upon himself our human nature. He knew within himself the human capacity for reaching the divine as well as the human capacity for completely missing the mark. As Saint Paul wrote, "For our sake he made him to be sin who knew no sin..." (2 Corinthians 5:21), and as the author of Hebrews wrote, "For we do not have a high priest who is unable to sympathize with our weaknesses, but we have one who in every respect has been tested as we are..." (4:15). Though Jesus did not sin, he well knew our human capacity for sin.

We are treading boldly into the territory of mystery, but we need a deeper awareness of what God through Jesus Christ has done for us, of how much God loves and cares for all creation, the imperfect as well as the perfect. And by exploring this mystery of God's love, we will begin to realize what it is we truly aspire to become.

ACKNOWLEDGMENTS

I want to offer sincere thanks to all the people who have encouraged me in completing this work. Their support, patience, and guidance have never ceased, and their honest comments and directions have been a constant source of inspiration.

Early in the 1980s I was one of several people invited as resource persons for a pilot class titled "Sickness and Healing in the Old and New Testaments" at Catholic Theological Union in Chicago. My lifelong interest in theology gained a direction that would ultimately lead to this book—my personal effort to create a local theology of persons with disabilities.

The example and inspiration of Donald Senior, C.P., and the late Carroll Stuhlmueller, C.P., who prepared and presented this pilot class, have ever provided inspiration and staunch support. They never failed to encourage my efforts with their prayers and assistance. I can never thank them adequately for their belief in me. Moreover, this pilot course has now become one of the foundational courses for graduate studies at CTU.

Other members of the faculty, sensing the direction my inquiries took, guided my exploration of the place of the disabled in the history of the Church and in the development of ethical concerns, especially my thesis director, Carolyn Osiek,

R.S.C.J. Finally, in Robert Schreiter's course on contextual-ization at CTU, I discovered the underlying theme that would bring all my studies into a clear focus: the beginning of under-standing how to approach a local theology of the disabled.

Many others have given their support by the trust they placed in me: the dean of the archdiocesan college seminary, who hired me to teach English and philosophy to future priests; the chair of the English department at Mundelein College, who hired me purely on the basis of my qualifications, liter-ally sight unseen; the chair of the theology department at Loyola, who provided me my first opportunity to teach theol-ogy; and my many, many students, who have placed their trust in my teaching and responded to me with respect as a teacher.

My children too, placing total trust in me as mother, brought home friends and invited them for meals and activities. All these have added to the verification of my life as a whole hu-man being. And always, always, the one constant support, my husband, the rock upon which I have placed the founda-tion of my life.

Many other persons with handicaps have supported me along the way and encouraged me by their own personal de-termination not to allow society and prejudice to imprison their talents. Such courage and steadfast faith have inspired me and challenged me to pursue my goals, and without their examples, my quest would have failed.

THE DISABLED
DISCIPLE

1

BACKGROUND

One of the great joys of our finite nature is that we are able to rediscover what has already existed for years. We are not unlike children playing a game, searching for hidden treasures that they know already exist and simply await discovery. We know that our God is a good God, and that the work of God's hand, creation, is a result of God's love. But from time to time we rediscover a certain facet of this wondrous gift of God, and in our enthusiasm we proclaim its discovery as something never realized before.

We also believe that the Church founded by Christ has always been concerned for the poor and the outcast, and when we turn our attention to reviewing the Church's original commitment, its essential foundation, we are both thrilled and humbled by the overwhelming power of this truth. From time to time we must pause and review the Church's involvement so that we may continue its work with renewed commitment and dedication.

Here, however, we intend to take a closer look at our Church's concern for our society's outcasts and marginalized members, our friends with disabilities, with a sincere desire to encourage this concern—to bring it up-to-date, so to speak.

THE SIGNS OF THE TIMES

When Pope John XXIII, in the early days of Vatican II, told us to "look to the signs of the times," he was simply reaching out to a principle clearly established by Jesus in his ministry. Jesus came, as the prophet Isaiah had announced, precisely to address the concerns of the poor, the captives, the disabled, the oppressed, and "...to proclaim the year of the Lord's favor" (Luke 4:19).

Jesus left us countless examples and directions of how we should apply his words about reaching out to others. He did this by the works he performed for the poor and imprisoned, for Gentile and Jew, for slave and free, for the men and women to whom he had been sent.

Pope John's actions and words throughout Vatican II also directed our attention out toward all humanity—to all in suffering and poverty—telling us that by looking to the signs of the times we would find the fields ripe for the harvest. He was responding to a growing concern for human rights throughout the world. Our twentieth century may well be remembered for this remarkable achievement: the concern and recognition of human rights on every level, in every guise, by every group, and this on a truly universal dimension. Whether this worldwide attention to the rights of all human beings first tangibly appeared in the secular domain or grew on the solid foundation of religious principles is of little matter. What is noteworthy is that it has come to birth in our own time.

Karl Rahner spoke of the universal Church. In embracing our common oneness, as Church and as world, we begin to glimpse what Rahner meant. Churches, along with other religious institutions, have begun establishing ministries for and with persons with various types of disability, persons whom we might well call the invisible minority. And in response to the increasing visibility of this minority, many ministries are now offering hope to a group that for too long has been over-looked, ignored, and discounted. So often in the past the choice seemed to be between patronizing these persons, thereby leaving them no dignity, or ignoring them, thereby leaving them in utter despair. Now we can take heart and celebrate because this either-or attitude seems to be opening up to a new choice, that of fashioning the kingdom of God in our midst.

SECULAR SOCIETY'S AWARENESS OF THE NEED FOR INCLUSION

We note that our secular brothers and sisters have long been involved in securing human rights and in providing the soothing balm of justice for all peoples. The American bishops acknowledged as much in their 1978 *Pastoral Statement of U.S. Catholic Bishops on Persons with Disabilities* (#6).

Throughout history, remarkable individuals have stepped forward to battle injustice, but our century is noteworthy for the rapid increase of organizations championing human dignity. They have often been at the forefront in advocating legal measures to effect the needed changes. The United Nations is one such organization, and it proclaimed 1981 as the International Year of the Disabled. But we must acknowledge the efforts that preceded this important event to put our discussion into its proper perspective.

In the United States, the Civil Rights Act of 1964 focused primarily on racial discrimination against African-Americans and soon led to demonstrations and further action that benefited other deprived groups.

In 1972 the Education Act focused on the rights of women in educational and employment areas, and laws prohibiting discrimination on the basis of age followed soon after.

The Rehabilitation Act of 1973 highlighted the needs of individuals with disabilities who were and are methodically denied employment and education, but its jurisdiction extended only to federally funded programs and institutions.

As the decade was drawing to a close, the Education of Handicapped Children Act of 1978, ensuring the rights of all children to adequate and appropriate education, demonstrated continued secular awareness.

Inspired by this proliferation of civil-rights laws, and by the results of public demonstrations and public concern, individuals with disabilities joined together in the eighties and nineties and established the Disability Rights Movement. After a decade of demonstrations and protests, in 1990 the Americans with Disabilities Act (the ADA) was signed into law, prohibiting discrimination not merely in federally funded institutions and programs but nationally, in five important areas: access to employment, access to public buildings, access to public accommodations, access to transportation, and access to communication services. Disability was given the same protection as race, religion, and gender.

Hopefully, legal protection will bring about unparalleled social change benefiting persons with disabilities.

Now that we have begun to protect the less fortunate among us, we can begin to discern more clearly who those people with disabilities really are and why they have been invisible for so long. Because people with disabilities are often also members of various other disadvantaged groups—identified by race, by sex, by ethnic origin, by age, by nationality, and so on—it is difficult to envision them as a distinctive group in themselves. The unfortunate result is that they remain invisible, and little if anything is actually accomplished on their behalf.

On the other hand, lumping together persons with very different disabilities is also a real danger. A strong group identity could result in a backlash, and we must all remain alert to prevent a return to unacceptable conditions, particularly when regress is disguised as economic necessity for all.

THE RELIGIOUS DIMENSION

Religious advocates of human rights are taking note of and encouragement from what others have accomplished in the secular sphere. To retreat now from what has been accomplished for people with disabilities would be a fatal blow for religious integrity as well as for the advancement of civilization, returning us to the ancient proscriptions of Leviticus, wherein the Chosen People were cautioned against allowing any male with a disability to offer sacrifice to God under pain of excommunication from the community: "No one of your offspring throughout their generations who has a blemish may approach to offer the food of his God" (Leviticus 21:17). Too long has the sting of this ancient curse poisoned the "sweet saving waters" of which Isaiah so tenderly sang:

> Ho, everyone who thirsts,
>   come to the waters;
> and you that have no money,
>   come, buy and eat!
> Come, buy wine and milk
>   without money and without price (Isaiah 55:1).

Now that God's saving love is emerging more clearly in both the sacred and the secular realms, we must never forget the shocking fact that at present more than 80 percent of disabled persons are either unemployed or underemployed, living on government subsidies and sinking ever further into despondency. Many of the individuals who make up this 80 percent are educated, well trained, willing, and capable of becoming full tax-paying citizens and participating parishioners, if the chance were given them. Now is the time to truly reform our societies and our Church, to prevent primitive, ungodly proscriptions from ever dominating our spirits and our world again.

2

THE EXPERIENCE
OF EXCLUSION

Generally speaking, persons with disabilities are not the first choices for significant positions in either the secular or the religious sphere. Exceptions do occur, but the exceptions we have seen are so unusual that we may well declare this generality as almost a premise based upon universal evidence.

This is an unfortunate waste because people can accomplish truly remarkable things with education, training, and opportunity. This is true of people with disabilites as well as temporarily able-bodied people (TABs). Some disabilities are more severe and limiting than others, and obviously, some tasks are out of the question for some people. For example, those who are blind or visually limited ought not aspire to driving a motor vehicle. Persons with significant hearing loss cannot presume to critique Placido Domingo or to evaluate the opening night of the Metropolitan Opera season. For each person with a disability, there is work of which he or she can become properly capable. People with disabilities may need some reasonable accommodation to do certain things. They may go about things differently, but sensitivity, imagination, and concern, coupled with the right guidance and adequate facilities, can bring about truly amazing results. As Christians, we would be very foolish to consign individuals to the outer realms of society before providing them the opportunity to shine in their own right.

THE HERITAGE OF PERSONS
WITH DISABILITIES

History provides rich examples of numerous great persons who have overcome enormous challenges.

Saint Paul was supposed to have had some serious disability—blindness, epilepsy—whatever "a sting in the flesh" means. But he boasted of his weakness and found strength in the very disability given him.

> Therefore, to keep me from being too elated, a thorn was given me in the flesh, a messenger of Satan to torment me, to keep me from being too elated. Three times I appealed to the Lord about this, that it would leave me, but he said to me, "My grace is sufficient for you, for power is made perfect in weakness."…Therefore, I am content with weaknesses, insults, hardships, persecutions, and calamities for the sake of Christ; for whenever I am weak, then I am strong (2 Corinthians 12:7–10).

Paul also wrote of it to the Galatians:

> You know that it was because of a physical infirmity that I first announced the gospel to you; though my condition put you to the test, you did not scorn or despise me, but welcomed me as an angel of God, as Christ Jesus. What has become of the goodwill you felt? For I testify that, had it been possible, you would have torn out your eyes and given them to me. Have I now become your enemy by telling you the truth? (4:13–16).

Paul's affliction did not take away from his tremendous ability as an apostle. Scholars have speculated as to the type and extent of Paul's "disability," but none deny that Paul bore with him his affliction as he carried out his ministry throughout the ancient world and eventually in Rome.

In our own time, we know persons with disabilities who are inspiring teachers, good parents, competent lawyers, even a world-renowned physicist. Stephen Hawking, now reduced to total physical disability and unable to speak, teaches while using an electronic device. He manages to get around by means of a wheelchair and continues to pursue his brilliant and original discoveries.

Despite the evidence, however, we never seem to advance past the stage of asking for proof upon proof.

THE LESSON OF SISYPHUS

Greek mythology tells of the great hero Sisyphus, the lover of humankind, who bestowed on us the gift of fire. For this tremendous generosity, he was doomed to the eternal punishment of having to roll an enormous boulder up a gigantic mountain. He would no sooner reach the pinnacle than down the huge burden rolled, consigning him to retrace his agonizing steps.

Like Sisyphus, far too many persons with disabilities do achieve their goals, do reach the pinnacle toward which they climb, only to have their next step questioned; or to receive for their efforts a pat on the shoulder, as one might stroke a friendly animal; or to receive a patronizing comment: "How wonderful you are! I almost forgot that you're disabled." It's like saying, "Once more, Sisyphus! We know you can do it."

PERSONAL EXPERIENCE

Since my own disability is blindness, I am alert to the many stereotypes and large amount of misinformation about this condition. Many people believe that most blind persons are born blind. That is simply not true. Blindness occurs for many reasons and is another condition that many people in our increasingly aging population may face. Many people lose their sight, totally or partially, from accidents or from diseases. In my case, I became blind when I was almost ten years old.

It came about on an early evening in late August when I had gone roller skating in the nearby rink and ended up on the bottom of a pileup with one of the skates hitting me in the head, putting pressure on the optic nerve. The inevitable began slowly at first, with splitting headaches, double vision, nausea, and, eventually, the loss of sight.

I've never been clear about my parents' knowledge of this accident at the skating rink because I remember not telling anybody about the fall. At home I said nothing about the headaches but prepared to return to school after Labor Day. But things began to be increasingly hard to overlook.

Music and art were my favorite subjects, and I was one of the two children from my school selected to enter a city-wide art contest. I was thrilled and made every effort to fulfill my responsibilities. The headaches were by then intense, and my vision seemed to be doing funny things. As I attempted to draw Daniel Boone for the contest in American history, I was confusing colors: red for brown, green for blue, and so on. Daniel Boone emerged from the paper with eyes red enough to draw the teacher's notice. I changed the red to brown, but then the sky and prairie took on odd colors, and she pointed this out to me as well.

At home, I frequently noticed that things were doubled:

two chairs where I knew there was only one, and two plates on the table where only one had been set.

My parents grew more worried, and we began interminable trips to religious shrines, petitioning for a miracle. Once, my father took me to the home in the old Italian neighborhood on the West Side of Chicago where my parents had lived when they were first married. We were trying white magic, which failed, and only then did the endless visits to doctors begin in earnest.

Finally—it seemed like years but was actually only a few weeks—school was forgotten, art contests were put aside, and I heard serious talk of hospitals and surgery. When all this had been accomplished and total blindness had descended, I returned home to complete my recovery.

Being the center of attention was enjoyable for a time. Gifts and cards and boxes of chocolates to cheer me up were fine. But soon my attention returned to the world I had once occupied.

RISING UP FROM THE FALL

I began to yearn for classes, for friends outside to play games with, for roller skates, and for all the things I had so recently been doing. I still longed to jump rope, play hopscotch, and find colorful weeds in the nearby prairie with my friends, whose voices I could hear from the confines of my home.

Perhaps people born blind are more conditioned to whatever lot they are given, some luckier than others, but I had not known anything but the life of a sighted child—going to school, playing with my friends, looking forward to dating, dancing, marrying, having children, and one day becoming a teacher or an artist.

Not too long after my surgery, the truant officer came to visit my mother, and when my mother told her what had happened to me, she advised doing nothing because, as she said, "What's the good of education in her condition?" Young as I was, this comment troubled me and festered inside, driving me to look for a way to express my intense reaction against this attitude, this lack of belief in my abilities. I was no Jane Eyre, no Oliver Twist seeking to go up against the uninformed strictures of society, but I sensed that the truant officer's dismissal was wrong.

MAINSTREAMING

When I joined the ranks of the blind, it never occurred to me that I would have to stop doing whatever I had been doing before my fall. I don't remember thinking that anything would be different for me except that I would have to learn different ways of doing what I had always done.

Once, hearing the kids outside playing—hopscotch, double dutch, something—I found a trophy my brother had won at a local carnival, a slender cane with a large die for a handle. Casting the die for freedom, as it were, I used the cane to keep me on the sidewalk as I walked along the edge and touched the grass or dirt with it. It worked fine, and I was excited by this little taste of freedom.

The voices of my playmates came nearer as I went along, but I could also hear what their mothers were saying to them: "Stay away from her or you might catch it"—alluding to my blindness as though it were measles or mumps.

As I reached the prairie where weeds blossomed in rich profusion, the first stone hit me. I was startled and stopped. More stones followed, and I found myself sliding down into the safety of the prairie for cover, seizing a few stones to fling back in retaliation. My father happened to look out the window, came quickly after me, and put an end to the stoning as well as to my self-initiated mobility training. I'm sure that the stones penetrated into my father's soul. He surely was far more hurt than I.

Two years passed before my parents realized how restless I was and how much I needed to get back into school. My mother sought help from the good Sisters of Providence at our parish elementary school and asked them if I might sit in on the classes. With their assistance, we discovered that the Chicago Board of Education had a program in place that consisted of several "braille rooms" in different areas, with special-education teachers, to which blind children were sent for instruction in writing and reading braille. There were three or four in the city, I think, and I was sent to one, confined to a room with other blind kids and a few braille writers. Carefully kept apart from "normal" kids, we were even locked in at midday while the teacher went out for lunch. That wasn't my style either.

The first thing these educators did was to administer an IQ test to place me properly. The test was in braille, which I did not yet know how to use. I failed miserably, so they placed me, at the age of twelve, in the first grade, reinforcing the impression that I was somewhat less than "normal."

The cane episode as well as this new experience taught me one thing: that getting back into the world and "mainstreaming" (though I had not learned that word yet) was the only way to go. I wanted the life toward which I thought I had been headed. Instead, I was being given the old poetic lie: O how good and how noble it is for blind children to accept society's concept of separate but scarcely equal education.

This was unacceptable. I wanted all that I had had before I went blind. Segregated living was simply not for me. As I would come to know, separate anything is never equal.

Was this a prompting of the Holy Spirit? Whatever its origin, this was a blessing for which I shall always be grateful.

By this grace, I sensed that mainstreaming would be the only way to live fully.

Gerard Manley Hopkins captured the exhilaration of conquering difficulties in his poem "The Windhover: To Christ our Lord," in which he described the joy, the joie de vivre of this little bird soaring upon the winds, overcoming obstacles.

> I caught this morning morning's minion,
>   kingdom of daylight's dauphin,
>   dapple-dawn-drawn Falcon, in his riding
>   Of the rolling level underneath him steady air, and striding
> High there, how he rung upon the rein of a wimpling wing
> In his ecstasy! then off, off forth on swing,
>   As a skate's heel sweeps smooth on a bow-bend:
>   the hurl and gliding
>   Rebuffed the big wind. My heart in hiding
> Stirred for a bird,—the achieve of,
>   the mastery of the thing!

Stumbling blocks will be found along any path, but when we keep the goal in sight, help will come to clear away obstacles. In my own case, guardian angels in various forms often materialized to encourage me, to flag me on through. One was a concerned substitute teacher who tutored me in math and other subjects I had missed while occupying my lowly seat in first grade. She had me properly tested and returned to an appropriate grade, and I was on my way.

Another was Bishop Bernard Shiel, known for his active social involvement, who happened to visit the public high school I was attending and, more like a fairy godmother than a guardian angel, asked me what he could do to help me out. As in the words of the psalmist, "out of the mouths of babes," I spontaneously poured forth my dreams to the bishop and told him of my wishes to attend a neighborhood Catholic high school for girls. My wish was granted, and the rest is history.

The Groves of Academe

Preconceptions seem to govern every attempt by a person with disabilities to enter the normal world. This unacceptable situation exists even in the realms of academe.

I once answered a phone call from Columbia College in Chicago, to which I had sent my résumé for a part-time teaching position. The committee liked what they read and telephoned me to set up an interview.

I had not mentioned anything other than pertinent, professional information in my résumé. However, as I came into the English Department office bustling with students asking questions and turning in assignments, I immediately became aware of a sensation in the air. Even before I introduced myself, I knew what the outcome of my interview would be.

The professor who interviewed me never returned my inquiry. So after several days of humiliating suspense, I pursued the results of the interview and was told that the position had been filled. That was simply not true. Thoroughly enraged at the lie, I took the college to court—and won.

I had in the meantime obtained a similar position, but I felt it necessary to make Columbia College aware that discrimination would not go unchallenged. One hopes that losing the lawsuit led the college to some reexamination of its criteria for employment.

Camelot: A Different Kind of Grove

On the other hand, from time to time a glimpse of the kingdom catches us by surprise and causes us to pause in wonder at the nearness of the reign of God.

A phone message reached me late one summer, advising me that the chair of the Department of English at Mundelein, a well-known women's college in Chicago, had just read my résumé and wanted to hire me to teach several courses. Burned before, I hesitated, girded up my loins, and returned the call.

"Yes," the chairperson assured me, "your qualifications suit us very well. You are our kind of professor. I have no time to interview you personally right now. Simply sign the contract, and we'll have coffee together after you teach your first class next week." And she hung up.

What to do? After Columbia and its incredible deceit, I was truly concerned. I phoned again to tell her that I would be using a guide dog to get around the campus. I am sure that this made her fully aware of the situation, but all I remember is a cheerful voice saying, "Oh, won't it be great to have a dog on campus. See you after your first class. Good-bye."

So it was. The totally unexpected day—the day of acceptance on the basis of my qualifications—was a day truly made by the Lord! Was this Camelot? Would the college doors open like the golden gates of heaven when I arrived, briefcase in hand, to begin teaching on that campus?

No. There was just a bustling swarm of females rushing in and out and up and down, many pouring into my class for the new semester. I was at home. I sensed that this was what Jesus meant when he said that the kingdom of God is among us.

OTHERS' EXPERIENCES

I was hearing about others who were seeking their rightful places in the sun, and one remarkable story bears repeating here.

A blind man I know, born in Israel, now a citizen of the United States, a leader in both the national and the international organizations of and for blind and visually impaired individuals, a graduate of the University of Chicago in political science and business administration, able to speak several languages fluently, applied for an opening at the U.S. State Department.

The government had to allow him to take the foreign-service exam, and to provide it in braille for his convenience, but the administrators were horrified when he passed it with an outstanding score. They readministered the exam with several restrictions, and once more the obstinate blind man passed it with flying colors.

After consultation and much serious discussion about access to classified materials, he was informed that he had to take the exam yet again. No problem. He passed again, and then the officials were really alarmed. What to do? Simple. They revised the exam, changed the rules regarding classified materials, and told him that there was no way they could allow anyone to assist him as a reader because the questions were classified. This would, unfortunately, exclude him from taking the newly designed exam. They were sorry, but those were the rules.

Undaunted, he won the assistance of a member of the U.S. House of Representatives from Minnesota, who began an appeal on his behalf. But only after protracted discussions and more alarms did the blind man finally achieve the position of overseas officer, for which he was and is eminently qualified. He has served with distinction in several foreign countries and is still an official representative of the U.S. government as an overseas officer.

Other similarly situated individuals joyfully heard of his achievement, took the exam, passed it, and are also presently employed by the State Department. Nothing has fallen apart. No foreign enemies have taken over our government. All is well, and a few qualified blind people are off the Social Security rolls and Supplementary Disability Income and have become contributing, tax-paying citizens.

Other individuals with other types of disabilities have taken heart of late, and with this inspiration have joined the ranks of the employed. Many people with disabilities are assuming roles as attorneys, professors, and business managers. One friend of mine who lost his sight as a college student when somebody put rubbing alcohol into his beer is a pharmacist at a large teaching hospital in Chicago.

Many are establishing families and caring for children and homes (when they can afford to purchase a home), and in general, things are improving. However, lest we think the kingdom exists in full splendor, we cannot neglect mentioning that a backlash against the ADA has become evident, as was noted in the *Chicago Tribune* early in 1995.

It reported that when the ADA was first passed in 1990, there was an immediate increase in the number of persons with disabilities seeking gainful employment. However, because employers and personnel administrators are still loath to take a chance or to use their imaginations, discrimination has simply become less obvious. It is easy to think of any number of reasons unrelated to disability not to hire a candidate.

The opposition has simply gone underground, and the word has gone out to would-be seekers of gainful employment. Many have ceased looking for appropriate positions, sensing that their day in the sun has grown very cloudy.

Most of us remain certain that if we hold on, God will once more prevail, and the kingdom will return to the land. Our God is a God of compassion and justice, and now, with law on our side as well, we will be able to bring more of God's kingdom into our very midst.

But how does the real world of Columbia College, of Mundelein College, and of the State Department—even under the ADA—mirror the world the New Testament envisions?

FELIX CULPA

At Easter we celebrate the fullness of God's redemption of human beings from the Fall. We sing that this fault, this fall from grace, this *culpa,* is the true antinomy for all believers. "For since death came through a human being, the resurrection of the dead has also come through a human being..." (1 Corinthians 15:21).

We sing that if Adam and Eve had not committed this original sin—whatever metaphorically we mean by "original sin"—we would not have the joy of rejoicing in Jesus' redemptive act. We rightfully celebrate this fault, for from it comes the resurrection of the dead. This is preeminently true for those who have risen from the darkness of disability. For me, the fall in that distant neighborhood skating rink, my *culpa* in the true sense, provided me with incalculable riches and opportunities. One certainly cannot casually claim that blindness, devastating trauma though it be, or any other illness or disability is good in itself. But we can certainly sing of the good that came from Jesus' crucifixion, of the *felicitas* that sprang forth for all Christians from the original *culpa* in the Garden of Eden. And so with disability. I knew not what lay in wait for me as a result of that indelible event in the neighborhood skating rink. But what I do know, what I do celebrate, is the remarkable series of events that have changed my entire life.

I was often discouraged, and I could have remained so. But I took heart from the achievements of others struggling on the way. And from those poets who offered refreshing words to restore my drooping spirits and remind me of God's inexplicable love for all people:

> Though thou with clouds of anger do disguise
> Thy face; yet through that mask I know those eyes,
> which,

Though they turn away sometimes
Never will despise.

John Donne

We followers of Jesus must also reflect seriously on the lessons of the New Testament. Jesus himself told us how we should act:

> "I will show you what someone is like who comes to me, hears my words, and acts on them. That one is like a man building a house, who dug deeply and laid the foundation on rock....But the one who hears and does not act is like a man who built a house on the ground without a foundation" (Luke 6:47–49).

The gospels should be our primary manual, and it is to them that we turn for our guidance and inspiration.

3

THE NEW TESTAMENT

Throughout the gospels, we read of Jesus' concern for the outcast. And in numerous parables, stories, and sayings he left us examples of how we ought to respond to the poor, to the disabled, and to people who are different from us. These examples are at the heart of the teachings—the *kerygma*—by which his disciples are to follow him in his "way." They are the grounding upon which his followers must build the kingdom.

Jesus' stated his platform clearly at the very beginning of his public ministry, in his inaugural address, as it were, to the assembled people in his hometown synagogue. He selected a passage from the prophet Isaiah who, living in a very primitive culture, centuries earlier, had offered a clear foreshadowing of Jesus' entire ministry. Reading from the scroll, Jesus proclaimed,

> "'The Spirit of the Lord is upon me,
>   because he has anointed me
>   to bring good news to the poor.
> He has sent me to proclaim release to the captives
>   and recovery of sight to the blind,
>   to let the oppressed go free,
> to proclaim the year of the Lord's favor'" (Luke 4:18–19).

Throughout his life Jesus continued to unroll that scroll at those very words—by breathing life into the words by the works he performed.

In Hebrew, the word *dabar* means both "word" and "work," depending upon the context in which it is used. In the life of Jesus, his words were his work: his *dabar* was one, a unified whole. The words he spoke, the proclamation he made at the outset of his ministry, were intrinsically part of his work.

We read in the prologue of the Gospel of John that "in the beginning was the Word, and the Word was with God, and the Word was God" (1:1). We know that the Gospel of John was written in Greek, and that the Greek word for "word" is *logos*. It seems a short step to join these two words, *dabar* and *logos*—which provides us with a most interesting connection between *word* and *work*. We participate in Jesus' ministry by following the examples he provided—in participating in the Word by the work we do—as Jesus is one with God.

We find this spirit of oneness compellingly described in the earliest writings of the New Testament, the letters of Saint Paul, in whom we encounter the essential characteristic of those who wish to be Jesus' followers. In writing to the Galatians, Paul recorded for us the central, dominant focus of a true Christian. We read in this letter, "There is no longer Jew or Greek, there is no longer slave or free, there is no longer male and female; for all of you are one in Christ Jesus" (3:28). By stressing that Jesus' followers must serve one another selflessly—must become one—Paul was simply writing down what Jesus had done throughout his brief ministry: become one with all people.

This spirit manifests itself in many significant ways in the gospels: There is salvation for all, even the Gentiles. There is concern for women, who were socially almost as disadvantaged as slaves. There is compassion for the sick and the disabled. And finally, there is Jesus' curing and healing on the Sabbath, in public opposition to the religious leaders, an antagonism that ultimately resulted in his death.

Some have ventured to compare Jesus' opposition to religious authorities with that of today's liberation theologians, whose priority is justice for the individual rather than preservation of the status quo.

Although our emphasis lies primarily with Jesus' interaction with disabled people, we must briefly reflect upon these other themes to place the consideration of the disabled in context.

CONCERN FOR FOREIGNERS

First, let us consider Jesus' outreach to foreigners, to the Gentiles, in the well-known story of the Good Samaritan.

A man fell among thieves who robbed him, stripped him, and left him at the side of the road for dead. Those who saw the wounded man passed by on the other side, so as not to get involved with police reports, or with those robbers, who just might still be nearby. A priest and a Levite hurried on by, averting their eyes, as if not to see what God saw. But a Samaritan, a foreigner, looked with the eyes of Jesus, approached the victim, and poured oil and wine over his wounds and bandaged them. Then he lifted him up on his own animal, took him to an inn, and cared for him. The next day he took out two silver coins and gave them to the innkeeper with the instruction, "'Take care of him; and when I come back, I will repay you whatever more you spend'" (Luke 10:30–35; author's paraphrase).

By telling stories in the Jewish *midrash* tradition, Jesus was illustrating what his listeners should do. And one might imagine Jesus turning to us as well and saying, "'Go and do likewise'" (Luke 10:37).

Jesus was moved with similar compassion on his own way to Jerusalem. He cured ten lepers and sent them to the priests.

> Then one of them, when he saw that he was healed, turned back, praising God with a loud voice. He prostrated himself at Jesus' feet and thanked him. And he was a Samaritan (Luke 17:15–16).

Jesus asked his listeners about the ten lepers whom he had cured. "'Were not ten made clean? But the other nine, where are they? Was none of them found to return and give praise to God except this foreigner?'" (Luke 17:17–19).

The meaning of such a question can hardly be misunderstood. Jesus reached out to all the marginalized, to the Gentiles, to sinners, to all who had fallen outside the realm of acceptability. This is the model he gave us, and no manual or resource book can replace what we already have as our basic text.

CONCERN FOR WOMEN

Again, it is Luke who told us that many women followed Jesus from Galilee, ministering to him, listening to his words, staying with him through the agony of the crucifixion. The same women were present at the empty tomb on Resurrection morning.

Though Luke's Gospel is rich with numerous examples of Jesus' concern for women, the Gospel of John provides us with two unique pericopes: the scene at the well in Samaria, where Jesus held a theological discussion with a person who was both Samaritan and a woman (John 4:4–42), and the scene with the woman taken in adultery (John 8:1–12).

Indeed, Jesus' concern for women runs through all four gospels and has sustained women through centuries of discrimination and injustice.

THE DISTINCTION BETWEEN
CURING AND HEALING

In several of the healing stories, Jesus distinguished between physical curing and spiritual healing. He stressed the importance of inner or spiritual healing before a merely physical curing. This is an important distinction and one that might be stressed in light of the oft-repeated belief that unless Jesus makes the blind see and the lame walk, they are not really loved by the son of God.

This belief surfaces in our own day when a perfect stranger, often a declared born-again Christian, announces to a person with disabilities, and to the ever-present bystanders, that if she really believed in Jesus, she would be cured. Such an attitude on the part of Christians is deplorable.

Ministers working with disabled persons must remember the gospels' distinction between curing the body and healing the soul. For example, as related in the Gospel of Mark, a paralytic man was let down through the thatched roof into the midst of the crowd surrounding Jesus.

> When Jesus saw their faith, he said to the paralytic, "Son, your sins are forgiven." Now some of the scribes were sitting there, questioning in their hearts, "Why does this fellow speak in this way? It is blasphemy! Who can forgive sins but God alone?" At once Jesus perceived in his spirit that they were discussing these questions among themselves; and he said to them, "Why do you raise such questions in your hearts? Which is easier, to say to the paralytic, 'Your sins are forgiven,' or to say, 'Stand up and take your mat and walk'? But so that you may know that the Son of Man has authority on earth to forgive sins"—he said to the paralytic—"I say to you, stand up, take your mat and go to your home" (Mark 2:5–11).

Jesus healed the deaf mute, he expelled demons, he restored vision and sound limbs as we just noted in the Gospel of Mark, but I would like to compare Jesus' curing of a blind man as reported in two separate pericopes: first, the narrative in the Gospel of Luke, and then the theologically quite different story as told in the Gospel of John.

Blindness is, many assert, the most frightening, the most objectionable of disabilities, so Jesus' interaction with blind people may offer us some insights into our own attitudes toward people with disabilities. And we may ask, what did Jesus have in mind as he cured the blind man, as in Luke, and again in John, as he went out looking for the man who was born blind and then cured, to engage him in rather serious theological discussion?

THE BLIND MAN: LUKE'S VERSION

Luke, the putative physician, presented a straightforward story of the curing of a blind man:

> As he approached Jericho, a blind man was sitting by the roadside begging. When he heard a crowd going by, he asked what was happening....Then he shouted, "Jesus, Son of David, have mercy on me!" Those who were in front sternly ordered him to be quiet; but he shouted even more loudly, "Son of David, have mercy on me!" Jesus stood still and ordered the man to be brought to him; and when he came near, he asked him, "What do you want me to do for you?" He said, "Lord, let me see again." Jesus said to him, "Receive your sight; your faith has saved you." Immediately he regained his sight and followed him, glorifying God...
> (18:35–43).

Here it seems that Jesus' primary concern was for the economic and social status of this blind beggar. Jesus said, "'Your faith has saved you.'" Saved him from what? From the economic and social situation he was in? No real job opportunities lay in wait for a blind man or woman in those days—or in any other days, for that matter. Jesus released this man from penury and social degradation so that he might reenter society, find work, and be treated with dignity and status. Perhaps the disciples and those who attempted to silence him could be likened to those who simply wish this minority—or any other—would make less noise and just collect their disability pittance, take up their stereotyped positions, and cease troubling the crowd of TABs passing them by. We must applaud the determination of the man that Mark called Bartimaeus and hope others in like situations today follow his example despite the disapproving crowds.

THE MAN BORN BLIND: JOHN'S VERSION

The entire ninth chapter of the Gospel of John is dedicated to a similar episode. However, in this account something more than a physical cure took place: the man born blind, doomed like Bartimaeus to the status of beggar, regained more than sight. He regained confidence and a certain unaccustomed spirit, and with this new spirit he actually engaged in theological repartee with the leaders of the community. His own parents, terrified of losing their membership in the local synagogue, disavowed their son.

Notice, this blind man did not approach Jesus and ask for healing: "As he walked along, he saw a man blind from birth. His disciples asked him, 'Rabbi, who sinned, this man or his parents, that he was born blind?'" (9:1–2). Jesus told his disciples that this man's blindness would somehow serve to give glory to God. Then Jesus made a paste from the earth, mixed it with his own spittle, anointed the blind man's eyes, and sent him to the pool of Siloam to wash off the mud.

When the man returned, seeing, he was bold to challenge the religious leaders who sought to indict Jesus for healing on the sabbath:

"...Do you also want to become his disciples?....Here is an astonishing thing! You do not know where he comes from, and yet he opened my eyes. We know that God does not listen to sinners, but he does listen to one who worships him and obeys his will. Never since the world began has it been heard that anyone opened the eyes of a person born blind. If this man were not from God, he could do nothing" (9:27–33).

The remarkable conclusion to this delightful episode is simple. It clearly implies that this man knew whence Jesus came, would become his disciple, would follow him, and would reach down through the darkness of discrimination to give hope and inspiration to others in his position, for why else would Jesus have taken such great care to search out afterward this inquisitive and very articulate beggar?

The two presentations—John's and Luke's—seem to reflect two different sets of concerns. John's story shows Jesus inviting this man to move from the abject state of a marginalized person to a full sharing in discipleship. This blind man perceived the real theological significance of his cure. When Jesus sought him out after the unseeing religious leaders ejected him from the temple, a most interesting dialogue took place:

"Do you believe in the Son of Man?" He answered, "And who is he, sir? Tell me, so that I may believe in him?" Jesus said to him, "You have seen him, and the one speaking with you is he." He said, "Lord, I believe." And he worshiped him (9:35–38).

I have come to think of this man as one of my spiritual ancestors, and when I visited the Holy Land, I made my own pilgrimage to the pool of Siloam, hoping to receive some of the spirit this man displayed in his reaction to Jesus.

Siloam.
Why there? Why were you sent?

The path was steep, the road too rough to climb,
And there no tour bus went.
The noonday hot, the canteen dry,
Along its treacherous slope I labored,
Not certain what I sought, nor what would find.

Some carried candles, some torches,
To guide precarious steps
Through Hezekiah's dank and narrow tunnel,
Where water flowed from Gihon's ancient spring.
I chose the other way, less trodden—
Down slippery slope and on down,
Down, down to Siloam's slimy surface.

Inside its stagnant waters children splashed and shouted,
As ancient children splashed and shouted
The day the blind man came with mud upon his face,
Sent by the stranger to wash.
What had he hoped to find? What did he seek?

He washed, and saw!
And more than saw—he followed.
Up out of the dungeons of despair,
Up from the ditches of disgrace,
Up out of centuries of Israel's shame and guilt
Into the light, the Son's light of discipleship.

He saw.
He more than saw. He followed.

CURING ON THE SABBATH

Again, Jesus went out to an ancient health spa, the pool
of Bethesda, territory of the pagan god Asclepius, to bring
God's saving, healing touch to those who lay in wait for new
life.

> After this there was a festival of the Jews, and Jesus went up to Jerusalem.
>
> Now in Jerusalem by the Sheep Gate there is a pool, called in Hebrew Beth-zatha [Bethesda], which has five porticoes....One man was there who had been ill for thirty-eight years....[Jesus] said to him, "Do you want to be made well?" The sick man answered him, "Sir, I have no one to put me into the pool when the water is stirred up; and while I am making my way, someone else steps down ahead of me." Jesus said to him, "Stand up, take your mat and walk." At once the man was made well, and he took up his mat and began to walk....
>
> Now the man who had been healed did not know who it was, for Jesus had disappeared in the crowd that was there. Later Jesus found him in the temple and said to him, "See, you have been made well! Do not sin any more, so that nothing worse happens to you." The man went away and told the Jews that it was Jesus who had made him well (John 5:1–15).

Oddly enough, this man who was cured seemed not to receive any increase of faith, but instead feared the Jewish leaders and went off to tell on Jesus so that he would not be thrown out of the synagogue.

The distinction here seems once again to be between curing and healing. The man paralyzed for thirty-eight years was physically cured but betrayed Jesus, preferring the security of the Jewish leaders and safety within the synagogue, within the status quo, to the precarious way of following Jesus.

The fact of curing is not necessarily followed by the grace of healing. If these men could accept Jesus' healing grace, they would know him as the Son of God. The man born blind did, and we rejoice with him; the man paralyzed for thirty-eight years did not and never would, and his physical condition may have changed, but his life had not.

The cure at Bethesda was on the Sabbath again, and the Jewish leaders, for this reason, "were seeking all the more to kill him, because he was not only breaking the sabbath, but was also calling God his own Father, thereby making himself equal to God" (John 5:18).

One final example of curing on the Sabbath is particularly revealing, for it heightened the opposition of the religious leaders against Jesus. It also shows Jesus' concern for women.

Teaching in a synagogue on the Sabbath, Jesus came upon a woman who had been crippled for eighteen years; she was bent over, completely incapable of standing erect. When Jesus saw her, he called to her and said, "'Woman, you are set free from your ailment'" (Luke 13:12).

The authorities were displeased with Jesus' concern for the sick and the disabled, whom he attended in preference to keeping the law, and in an almost ridiculous manner scolded the persons just cured.

> "There are six days on which work ought to be done; come on those days and be cured, and not on the sabbath day." But the Lord answered him and said, "You hypocrites! Does not each of you on the sabbath untie his ox or his donkey from the manger, and lead it away to give it water? And ought not this woman, a daughter of Abraham whom Satan bound for eighteen long years, be set free from this bondage on the sabbath day?" (Luke 13:14–16).

Despite all, Jesus was true to the priorities he proclaimed at the beginning of his ministry in the synagogue of Nazareth. As he summed it up, "'Those who are well have no need of a physician, but those who are sick; I have come to call not the righteous but sinners to repentance'" (Luke 5:31–32).

These are rich didactic examples of how Jesus fulfilled his inaugural promises to bring glad tidings to the poor, to cure the sick, and to free the oppressed. We must use his life and works and words as models in our own ministries.

4

FOUNDATIONS

In the Epistle to Timothy we read,

> ...God did not give us a spirit of cowardice, but rather a spirit of power and of love and of self-discipline.
>
> Do not be ashamed, then, of the testimony about our Lord...but join with me in suffering for the gospel, relying on the power of God, who saved us and called us with a holy calling, not according to our works but according to his own purpose and grace....Hold to the standard of sound teaching that you have heard from me, in the faith and love that are in Christ Jesus. Guard the good treasure [the deposit of faith] entrusted to you, with the help of the Holy Spirit living in us (2 Timothy 1:7–9, 13–14).

Let us now turn to this "good treasure," the *depositum fidei,* to which Paul referred, to discover if we may, indeed, found a theology of inclusion on what the Church we believe Jesus came to establish has made of Jesus' Good News.

THE MAGISTERIUM

Since certain doctrines of our faith are not specifically described in the Scriptures, the Church, as the institution established by Jesus, exercises the authority, when it meets in council, to elaborate elements of the creed we all believe, such as creation, the Incarnation, the Resurrection, the Redemption, and the eschaton. The seeds of our beliefs are present in Scripture; but the tenets of our creed were the focus of development and serious elaboration by the early councils, were subjected to centuries of debate and discussion, frequently caused dissension and even schism among early believers, and now are accepted as part of our tradition, upon which our faith securely rests.

The Roman Catholic Church, the Eastern Orthodox Church, and all the so-termed "high" churches—Lutherans, Anglicans, Episcopalians, and others—acknowledge the early Church councils of Nicaea, Ephesus, and Chalcedon, and some non-Catholic churches even acknowledge the work of the Roman Catholic councils up to and including Vatican II.

We will stress the doctrines that bear specifically on our theological consideration and how they are concerned with the place of the disabled.

FOUNDATIONS

Creation

We understand that God created all things, and with this understanding, our faith necessarily holds that all things are good, that there is no distinction between the sacred and the profane in any essential sense. "And it was so. God saw everything that he had made, and indeed, it was very good" (Genesis 1:30–31).

Our purpose, however, is to focus on how disabled individuals, imperfect creatures who yet must be seen as "very good," reflect the all-perfect Being we call God. Some have termed the disabled "children of a lesser god," but where do these children figure in the doctrine of creation. If some of creation is not perfect, must we conclude either that God is less than omnipotent or that there is a dual principle of creation—some Manichean spirit?

Not necessarily. May not the presence of imperfection be a vibrant indication that something more, something radically transcendent to our finite natures, lies just beyond? Can't we see that this apparent divine aberration does not deflect God's beauty, God's ineffable perfection, but simply evidences our lack of imagination, our limited finite capabilities? Do we miss the mark by trying to place ourselves on the same analogous level as the divine? Any assertion that our finite perfection is in some way analogous to divine perfection seems to be taking us perilously near blasphemy. In this type of presumption—placing any creature on the same level as God—does sin originate.

In the *Summa Theologica*, Thomas Aquinas used an argument from gradation to illustrate that God's perfection, though analogous to ours, is infinitely beyond anything we, as finite beings, can ever comprehend:

> But "more" and "less" are predicated of different things according as they resemble in their different ways something which is the maximum....Therefore there must also be something which is to all beings the cause of being, goodness, and every other perfection; and this we call God (I ii 3).

Aquinas's argument is our theological expression of how the imperfect may in some analogous way reflect the perfection of the Supreme Being we call God.

Perhaps poetry more effectively sees beyond the cumbersome nature of our human thoughts to penetrate to the heart of what Jesus did for us in his Incarnation. W. H. Auden set aside our laborious articulations and masterfully captured this incredible gift in "For the Time Being":

Redeem for the dull the
Average Way,
That common ungifted
Natures may
Believe that their normal
Vision can
Walk to perfection.

The Incarnation

One side of the early Arian controversies about Jesus' nature, centered in the school of Antioch among the adherents of Apollinarius, maintained that Christ had to be totally free of the corruption to which the flesh is heir. These intellectual, dedicated Christians argued that if Christ's nature were like that of Adam, it could not expiate the sin of our primal parent.

The Antiochene school used the term *prosopon,* which refers to the outward appearance of a person possessing two natures. Briefly, Christ, the Word, put on human nature as Greek actors donned theatrical masks.

Other equally dedicated, intellectual Christians held other views. The Alexandrians and the Cappadocians held that Christ's nature had to be fully human—he had to possess the fullness of human nature—for him to redeem human beings. Christ's humanity and Christ's divinity, for these believers, were equally real.

By the fifth century, this question about Christ's nature had puzzled the early Church for a long time and had suffered through many various interpretations, but the question was not to be resolved without a serious tremor in the Church's unity: a schism in 431–33. And evidence of Antiochene theology exists in certain Eastern Christian churches to this day.

To create a new theology of the disabled, the doctrine of the nature of Christ is of fundamental importance, for it is the very grounding of this emerging theology. If, as some have claimed, Jesus was not truly human but only appeared to be—

if he, so to speak, put on human nature like donning a mask that was not intimately part of him—his suffering an ignominious death reserved to criminals would have no significance for those whom we call outcasts.

We Catholics, on the other hand, assert that Jesus, second person of the Blessed Trinity, took human nature upon himself, so as to have the same nature as all of those others who are rejected and scorned. The outcasts, specifically disabled people, know that Jesus was like us, rejected, lowly, and held of little account.

With profound gratitude we note that Isaiah's Songs of the Suffering Servant captured the likeness we claim with Jesus. To paraphrase Isaiah,

> There was in him (in her, in me) no stately bearing to make us look at him (at her, at you, at me), nor appearance to attract us to him (to her, to them, to you). He was (she was, they were) spurned and avoided by men (and women), and we have bestowed on him (on her, on them) the name, a man (a woman) of suffering and accustomed to infirmity (Isaiah 53:2–3).

Paul used many of the same images in his letter to the Philippians:

> Let the same mind be in you that was in Christ Jesus,
>   who, though he was in the form of God,
>   did not regard equality with God
>   as something to be exploited,
>   but emptied himself,
>   taking the form of a slave,
>   being born in human likeness.
>   And being found in human form,
>   he humbled himself
>   and became obedient to the point of death—
>   even death on a cross (2:5–8).

The Redemption

Here we must reflect on the ultimate consequence of the Incarnation: our redemption.

Jesus did not come to challenge our capabilities to analyze why the Word was made flesh, with all the attendant theological ramifications, but to save us by dying in his human nature and then rising from the dead. We believe that we were indeed buried with him through baptism into death, so that, just as Christ was raised from the dead by the glory of God, we too might live in newness of life. "For if we have been united with him in a death like his, we will certainly be united with him in a resurrection like his" (Romans 6:5).

And we also believe that we are united with him in his identification with the suffering, the sinners, the outcasts. It is specifically this total identification of Jesus with the outcasts that is scandal to some but inexpressible glory to others. This is the focus of our Christology, the theological significance of the fact that Jesus, in his participation in our human nature, identified with us.

The Eschaton

Finally, in our development of a theology of the disabled, we turn to a consideration of the last things, the eschaton. When we speak of the eschaton, we speak of the future, the not-yet. This expectation, this desire of the human heart, distinguishes human beings from all other creatures in the universe. We can reflect upon a time when our finite existence will cease to be.

Atheistic existentialists find the thought of that future nothingness utterly agonizing. For them, life without hope ceases to have any importance. In Albert Camus's *The Plague*, Dr. Rioux, a humanistic, atheistic existentialist, demonstrates a total dedication to relieving human suffering, to filling the void, to providing some reason for living and a way of not thinking about the nothingness that awaits after death.

For those of us who believe in life after our physical death, the eschaton assumes a crucial importance in our decisions about how we are to live here and now. Death fails to deliver us into the hands of despair. Not fearing physical death, we may pursue life with the vigor and intensity worthy of God's children. We may begin to carry out the Christian way that Jesus came to show us. We may dedicate ourselves with the enthusiasm of those who know that the kingdom of God is already but not yet, and we can live out to the fullest what the kingdom is all about: justice for the poor, freedom for the enslaved, forgiveness for sinners, and all the Good News Jesus proclaimed at the outset of his ministry.

We must not think of eschatology as simply a reflection on the last things, something far off in the future, but we must understand that the seeds of the future are contained in the present, in the way in which we live in the kingdom that Jesus proclaimed was already here.

Martin Heidegger put this well when he said that the future of human beings cannot be separated from the human being's "being-in-the-present" (cited in Cone, 242). This articulation of a theological perspective of eschatology cannot entertain futuristic speculations of apocalyptic revelations; but in the full light of our beliefs in what Jesus did when he took upon himself our human nature—that is, raising human nature to a new dignity—we must assert that the kingdom of God already lives in our midst, though in a most incipient form. We can truly assert, boldly, that it is already but not yet.

Lest some theological wag cast a critical eye upon these hopes as merely "pie in the sky when you die," I hasten to affirm trust in the ultimate reconciliation, when all polarities shall find total resolution, when the final swords shall be at last beaten into plowshares, when the haves shall welcome the have-nots, when the outcasts shall be united to the outcasters, when we are all at last at peace. As evidence for this future of true peace *(shalom)*, of wholeness, we hold up the incremental victories of the oppressed, who in the midst of their sufferings have the tenacity to hope, for they have seen something beyond their mortality, for they have heard whispers of eternity and will not be deluded into the fallacy that finite being is all that ever will be.

We must understand that to consider the Incarnation, the Resurrection, the Redemption, and the Eschaton separately is merely part of the process of exploring how a theology of the disabled may be solidly founded upon truths fundamental to our faith. They may be seen as distinct events in the life of Jesus, certainly, but they represent a totality in a far more essential way.

Now, perhaps the greatest challenge is to demonstrate how disabled individuals figure in the understanding of these mysteries as publicly expressed in the life of the Church. How do disabled individuals become threads woven into a seamless tapestry? Without these essential threads, the entire tapestry of our faith unravels.

5

PUBLIC STATEMENTS OF THE CHURCH

The Church, established by Jesus Christ for the explicit purpose of carrying on his ministry in the world under the guidance of the Holy Spirit, has aptly been called a sacrament to the faithful. And we believe that grace flows through the Church, that it is one of the chief agents by which the faithful may receive God's grace.

In the case of disabled individuals, and of other outcasts too, we must ask whether this grace has been flowing from the Church as abundantly as the healing waters flowing down upon the parched earth of which the prophet Isaiah spoke:

> For waters shall break forth in the wilderness,
>   and streams in the desert;
> the burning sand shall become a pool,
>   and the thirsty ground springs of water... (35:6–7).

The Church has published many good words about its good intentions toward persons with disabilities. Words are not lacking. Words are not the problem. But like Polonius questioning Hamlet in Shakespeare's tragedy, we must ask of these words, "But what is their meaning?" And what is their result?

The Church's good words, by themselves, can be likened to the dead bones in the book of Ezekiel. Only when the Spirit is breathed into them will they rise up, join together, and begin to walk about as the Mystical Body of Christ, doing the work of his hands and feet, and bringing the kingdom of God into real existence.

THE EARLIER DOCUMENTS

The official social positions of the Church are usually expressed in encyclicals, the chief means by which public statements on dogma and morals are announced to the entire worldwide community. In surveying almost an entire century of these social documents, from Pope Leo XIII's *Rerum Novarum* up until the American bishops' *Pastoral Statement on Persons with Disabilities,* we find no specific mention of individuals with disabilities. Only by reading into the spaces, the lacunae, the erasures, may one read into these official pronouncements the Church's concern for the handicapped—the same phenomenon women recently have remarked as they study and reflect upon the Hebrew Scriptures.

Pope Leo XIII wrote at the end of more than a century of economic and social upheaval. There had been political revolutions in America and in France; Russia was on the brink of social change; Italy and Germany were awakening to a sense of nationhood. The elimination of serfdom in Russia and then of slavery in the United States, the ongoing struggle of women for human dignity and equality, and many other social movements demanded change.

The industrial revolution had taken such hold after 1832 that poets and writers such as Charles Dickens and George Eliot in England and Leo Tolstoy and Fyodor Dostoevsky in

Russia, to name but a few, were turning their attention from romanticism to the more exciting consideration of social justice and human rights. At the approach of the new century, Leo XIII barely had time to jump aboard the bandwagon. To the glory of the Church, and hopefully to its ultimate salvation, Leo did, and his pronouncements have reverberated down through the twentieth century.

Rerum Novarum (On the Condition of Labor) appeared in 1891. Pope Leo realized that a mighty throng of beleaguered industrial workers was rushing past—and away from—the pope and the Church. Nevertheless, one must not minimize the historical and social significance of this document, which represents a watershed in the history of the Church's involvement in the real earthly problems of the people of God: *Rerum Novarum* proved to be the forerunner of a series of pronouncements that continue to the present.

In *Rerum Novarum,* Leo XIII wrote of the harmony of the human body. In nature, he explained, all things work together for the good of the whole.

> Just as the symmetry of the human body is the result of the disposition of the members of the body, so in a state it is ordained by nature that these two classes should exist in harmony and agreement, and should, as it were, fit into one another so as to maintain the equilibrium of the body politic (#15).

Surely this image of the wholeness of the body cannot be seriously considered without reading into it the role of disabled members within this harmonious structure.

Leo XIII also commented on the role of the state in intervening on behalf of oppressed workers:

> Still, when there is a question of protecting the rights of individuals, the poor and helpless have a claim to special

consideration. The richer population have many ways of protecting themselves, and stand less in need of help from the state; those who are badly off have no resources of their own to fall back upon, and must rely chiefly on the assistance of the state (#29).

Obviously, one might read into this expression of papal concern the view that the disabled, having fewer resources of their own to fall back upon than anyone else in society, are preeminently entitled to rely on the assistance of the state.

As we perceive it today, *Rerum Novarum* seems to have been testing the troubled waters somewhat gingerly. (One might term it an encouragement to the rich to exercise an "option for the poor.") Many decades would pass before the leaders of the Church would publicly proclaim their own option for the poor in Medillin, Colombia, in 1968. But we cannot overlook *Rerum Novarum*'s powerful effect throughout the first half of the twentieth century.

In his turn, we may infer, Pope Pius XI would have included the disabled in his 1931 *Quadragesimo Anno:*

> ...bodily labor which was decreed by divine providence for the good of man's body and soul even after original sin, has too often been changed into an instrument of perversion: for dead matter leaves the factory ennobled and transformed, whereas men are there corrupted and degraded (cited in *Mater et Magistra,* #242).

Anyone who has lived among or known disabled individuals has seen the pitiable conditions that have been forced upon them because of a lack of training, of concern, of encouragement, and of significant participation in the management of their own lives. Those imprisoned within the walls of "sheltered workshops" or hidden away in back rooms have in many cases been "there corrupted and degraded."

Pope Pius XII spoke of every individual not as a merely

passive, permissive element in a just social order but as its very foundation and, indeed, its end:

> That perpetual privilege proper to man, by which every individual has a claim to the protection of his rights, and by which there is assigned to each a definite and particular sphere of rights, immune from all arbitrary attack, is the logical consequence of the order of justice willed by God (Christmas Message, 1942; cited in *Pacem in Terris,* #26–27).

> The human individual, far from being an object, as it were a merely passive element in the social order, is in fact, must be and must continue to be its subject, its foundation and its end (Christmas Message, 1945; cited in *Pacem in Terris,* #26–27).

Surely, if pressed, Pius XII would have included disabled people as an important part of any social order.

Finally, Pius XII reflected upon how the neglect of its disadvantaged members would affect a society: It is a "monstrous masterpiece" of this age, he wrote, "to have transformed man, as it were, into a giant as regards the order of nature, yet, in the order of the supernatural and the eternal, to have changed him into a pygmy" (Christmas Message, 1953; cited in *Mater et Magistra,* #243).

While we recall the statements of Leo XIII, Pius XI, and Pius XII with the greatest of approbation, we find ourselves left to surmise that they were including the disabled among those individuals who have a claim to full human rights. As the editors of *Renewing the Earth* (a collection of papal encyclicals published in 1977) perceived, these popes recognized "in the productive potential of modern industrial society the possibility of reducing human misery, and eradicating the curse of poverty, and freeing all persons for a more responsible possession of their lives and history" (p. 42).

MORE RECENT DOCUMENTS

Pope John XXIII's first encyclical, *Mater et Magistra (The Social Concerns of the Church)*, was published in 1961 upon the occasion of the dual anniversary of *Rerum Novarum* and *Quadragesimo Anno*. Pope John was a man uniquely aware of his position in time, and he was also aware that the Church was at a crucial juncture in the social leadership of the world. In this encyclical he wisely told us, echoing Jesus' words, that we must look to "the signs of the times." He perceived that in the post–World War II chaos the Church could no longer set itself apart from the concerns of the world but needed to be completely involved in and aware of the situation of the people it was committed to save. The Church, we agree, is in the world and must definitely be part of it and all its problems.

Pope John hoped to impress upon the world that a just sharing in the fruits of progress, a truly just wage, would bring about "a breakdown of class differences and the distributions of goods according to the norms of justice so that every one in the community can develop himself" (#46).

The tone of the document is optimistic, open, outward looking, and one searches it for glints of a concern for the disabled. One looks to such a document with hope—for some disapproval of the typical "sheltered shop," where the local version of a "just wage" is rarely equal to a "wage sufficient to lead a life worthy of man and to fulfill family responsibilities properly" (#71).

In any case, *Mater et Magistra* laid a solid foundation for the documents that were to follow and was the precursor of a newly evidenced concern for all people—in short, for the human rights of all people. Many at that time perceived it as a milestone on the path to a more just society.

Soon thereafter, in the fall of 1962, the world was poised

on the brink of nuclear war between the Soviet Union and the United States—a war that would have destroyed the most basic right that humankind possesses: life itself. At the height of the Cuban Missile Crisis, Pope John published *Pacem in Terris*. In it, he delineated his perception of the rights inherent in humankind's very nature, beginning with

> ...the right to life, to bodily integrity, and to the means that are suitable for the proper development of life; these are primarily food, clothing, shelter, rest, medical care, and finally the necessary social services. Therefore, a human being also has the right to security in cases of sickness, inability to work, widowhood, old age, unemployment, or in any other case in which he is deprived of the means of subsistence through no fault of his own (#11).

More clearly than any previous statement, *Pacem in Terris* included the disabled by addressing sheltered shops, supplementary subsistence insurance, and other social palliatives.

But the switch in emphasis from encouraging to demanding a more just society was about to occur. The Church had but to look at the United States to see a nation coming to grips with patterns of discrimination and exclusion that dated from its origins. Dissatisfactions with the status quo burst forth with such vigor in the sixties that they continue to influence us today. Despite the often violent opposition to full rights for its black citizens, the United States was moving inexorably toward the passage of the Civil Rights Act of 1964. Meanwhile, Pope John was discussing the content of *Gaudium et Spes (The Constitution on the Church in the Modern World),* which alarmed conservatives in Rome during the earlier stages of Vatican II.

It seems evident that forces for change could be halted in neither sphere of influence and that the wall between the Church and the world would inevitably become even more porous. *Gaudium et Spes* opened with the observation that

> The joys and the hopes, the griefs and the anxieties of the
> men of this age, especially those who are poor or in any
> way afflicted, these are the joys and hopes, the griefs and
> anxieties of the followers of Christ. Indeed, nothing genu-
> inely human fails to raise an echo in their hearts. For theirs
> is the community composed of men (#1).

If *Mater et Magistra* advised us to look to the "signs of the
times," *Gaudium et Spes* represented a focusing on what was
happening in the secular world, specifically in the spheres of
economics, politics, war, human rights, and marriage and family. The Church was simply acknowledging the obvious fact
that Christians live in the world and are definitely part of it.

But even *Gaudium et Spes* did not deal specifically with the
disabled, although frequent mention was made of the need to
be concerned with every group living in society. The encyclical advised, "Let everyone consider it his sacred obligation to
esteem and observe social necessities as being among the primary duties of modern man" (#30). It also noted that "each
nation develops the ability to express Christ's message in its
own way. At the same time, a living exchange is fostered between the Church and the diverse cultures of people" (#44).

This notion takes on a new, breathtaking scope in view of
an earlier statement in *Gaudium et Spes*:

> ...as a result the common good, that is, the sum of those
> conditions of social life which allows social groups and their
> individual members relatively thorough and ready access
> to their own fulfillment, today takes on an increasingly uni-
> versal complexion and consequently involves rights and
> duties with respect to the whole human race (#26).

This extension of the concept of the common good to all humankind reveals Pope Leo XIII's comment—that the harmony
in society must be that of the body as a whole—in an entirely
new light.

Thus, *Gaudium et Spes* followed *Mater et Magistra* and *Pacem in Terris* in tone and spirit, but perhaps represented a more developed consideration of justice. And Pope Paul VI's encyclicals about human dignity broadened the scope of previous papal social-justice writings to include the global community. His *Populorum Progressio* addressed primarily the adjustment of balances that must come to exist on a global scale. He expressed the Christian imperative of helping "particularly the development of those peoples who are striving to escape from hunger, misery, endemic diseases and ignorance; of those who are looking for a wider share in the benefits of civilization and a more active improvement of their human qualities" (#1). Obviously, disabled persons in ever larger numbers are among those peoples of the Third World, but the encyclical does not deal with them as a defined group.

A continued search for evidence of a specific concern for the disabled brings us to April 1981 and Pope John Paul II's encyclical on work, *Laborem Exercens*. There our current pope addressed the importance of work, pointing out that he was reflecting the themes of the first chapter of *Gaudium et Spes*. He wrote,

> ...as a person, man is therefore the subject of work. As a person he works, he performs various actions belonging to the work process; independently of their objective content, these actions must all serve to realize his humanity, to fulfill the calling to be a person that is his by reason of his very humanity (#23).

But such noble ends are impossible for countless disabled persons who have never been provided the proper training, education, skills, or opportunities to fulfill their own unique calling as human beings, nor are they provided work in line with this noble objective.

These documents championed human rights and dignity,

but none explicitly addressed the particular needs of disabled people. Despite the thousands of good words written and spoken, people with disabilities had to wait until the 1980s to catch a glimmer of waters breaking forth in the wilderness, and streams in the desert, of burning sands becoming pools, and thirsty ground springs of water.

6

DOCUMENTS ON PERSONS WITH DISABILITIES

Today the Church faces chaotic times, and the marginalized look to it for leadership. As in Pope Leo's time, the Church once again has a choice: immersing itself fully in this new tide of discontent, or risking being drowned out by those who would fill this void, whether secular powers or liberation theologies.

Finally, at the end of the twentieth century, religious leaders are turning their attention more specifically to the plight of persons with disabilities. Let us examine some of these modern manifestoes to determine how they deal with the concerns of the invisible minority.

THE U.S. BISHOPS' PASTORAL STATEMENT ON PERSONS WITH DISABILITIES

On November 16, 1978, the *Pastoral Statement of U.S. Catholic Bishops on Persons with Disabilities* was published. The waters of change washing through so many areas of our society had at long last reached the disabled, acknowledging them as a specifically identifiable group with definable concerns within the social awareness of the Church.

The bishops pointed out that Jesus came to the poor, the suffering, and the outcasts, and that in following his example, the Church has always been concerned with and aware of the handicapped and has rendered them signal service down through the ages. But as the bishops acknowledged, the Church had to change its focus, from its longstanding reliance on charity and custodial care to the creation of an awareness of dignity and value. To their credit, the bishops admitted, "…in a spirit of humble candor, we must acknowledge that at times we have responded to the needs of some of our disabled people only after circumstances or public opinion have compelled us to do so" (#6). In a later paragraph, they also mentioned pertinent legislation as well as other evidences of concern for the disabled on the part of the civil government. Their candor is indeed Ghandiesque. According to legend, Mahatma Ghandi was once overheard to say, as a huge throng of people rushed on past him, "There go my people, and I must follow them, because I am their leader." Similarly, the Church has now to catch up with secular society.

The bishops clearly recognized that the Church, as well as civil society, must continue to provide aid and services to the disabled but must never forget that providing such support is itself a privilege. "When we extend our healing hands to others," they pointed out, "we are healed ourselves" (#6).

But the most important aspect of this historic public statement is that it specifically set out to bring the disabled within the purview of John XXIII's vision, cited from *Pacem in Terris*:

> In an ordered and productive community, it is a fundamental principle that every human being is a person…[One]

has rights and duties…flowing directly and spontaneously from [one's] very nature. These rights are therefore universal, inviolable, and inalienable (#9).

To this end, the assembled bishops called "upon people of good will to reexamine their attitudes toward their disabled brothers and sisters and promote their well-being, acting with the sense of justice and the compassion that the Lord so clearly desires" (#1). It had become clear that

what disabled individuals need, first of all, is acceptance in this difference that can neither be denied nor overlooked. No acts of charity or justice can be of lasting value to persons with disabilities unless they are informed by a sincere understanding love that penetrates the wall of strangeness and affirms the common humanity underlying all distinction (#3).

"The wall of strangeness" of which the bishops wrote might well be crumbling. But the centuries of failure that allowed this wall to be built and to exist are in themselves a severe judgment against those who claimed to be followers of that all compassionate Lord, who did not turn away his face but took upon himself that very "strangeness" of which the bishops wrote, from which they too often turned away.

Addressing the role of the disadvantaged within the Church itself, the bishops advised that we "must reach out to welcome gratefully those who seek to participate in the ecclesial community.…The Church finds its true identity when it fully integrates itself with these 'marginal' people, including those who suffer from physical and psychological disabilities" (#12).

Perhaps what people secretly fear, and what they outwardly pity, is their own vulnerability, their own dark shadows. Perhaps people subliminally dread meeting their own Doppelgänger in this deaf-mute, in this twisted individual in the wheelchair, in this blind man with the blank stare.

It is not uncommon for people unconsciously to abhor and even resent individuals with disabilities, for handicapped persons are like subliminal mirrors reflecting one's own potentialities—what anyone might become—and we understandably reject this unacceptable possibility, avoiding the fact that all of us are merely temporarily able bodied.

But the bishops went further and stated that "disabled individuals bring with them a special insight into the meaning of life, for they live—more than the rest of us, perhaps—in the shadow of the cross" (#13). One must strongly reject such an overgenerous assessment. In truth, experience clearly reveals that disabled persons, like others, wax hot and cold. Many undoubtedly do "forge virtues such as courage, patience, perseverance, compassion and sensitivity" (#13). Others lack these qualities quite as thoroughly as do their temporarily able bodied brothers and sisters. Disabled people are, after all, human, and placing them on some sort of pedestal may be as effective a form of exclusion as any other.

However, the bishops quite sensibly went on to add that handicapped people are quite capable of being, and ought to be, consulted on how a community is to accommodate them. For example, all across the country, thousands of curbs have been cut and modified (at enormous expense) to accommodate the passage of persons in wheelchairs. These same curbs, however, provide the visually impaired using canes a way of knowing where the sidewalk ends and the street begins. In a moment of distraction, a person traveling with a white cane or dog-guide can easily find him- or herself in the middle of traffic because no curb was there to indicate the end of the sidewalk. Consultation with the visually impaired might have suggested that curb cuts be placed off to one side, thus accommodating both disabilities.

Such examples emphasize the need for broad consultation, for inclusion in the everyday activities of living. (I wonder whether the bishops consulted with a representative number of disabled persons while preparing their *Pastoral Statement on Persons with Disabilities.*)

In 1985 the American bishops published their pastoral letter on war and peace and shortly thereafter took up the next most pressing concern of their children living in the world: the economy.

However, when the American bishops published their *Pastoral Letter on the Economy* in 1986, they failed to identify the disabled as a group with special economic needs and deserving of special consideration. In the paragraphs dedicated to unemployment—in our own country and in the world at large—no mention was made of the astonishing and intolerable fact that unemployment among the disabled population in the United States has been estimated to run as high as 80 percent. This figure includes the blind, the deaf, the otherwise physically disabled, as well as the mentally and emotionally disabled, but does not include those out of the labor market because of age. Nor does it take into account the fact that many persons with disabilities who have jobs are underemployed or very poorly paid.

Not only is this shameful, but it is bad economics. Joseph Shapiro's recent book *No Pity* provides appalling statistics on the very high cost of warehousing disabled people in custodial institutions compared with the low cost of "mainstreaming" them. It would be far more economical, as well as more Christian, to train disabled people for and employ them in jobs that will support them, than to put them out of sight in nursing homes, mental hospitals, or sheltered shops.

In their pastoral, the bishops repeated their plea that economic planning must aim at the fulfillment of basic human needs, must include the poor and the vulnerable, and must consider the effect that economic policies have on families. The disabled must be specifically included in all these areas.

They are persons with special basic needs, as the encyclicals clearly noted. They are certainly among the poor and are more vulnerable than most by reason of their physical as well as their economic status. They, as individuals, are frequently not able to maintain their families in a respectable dignity because of their lowly status in the economic sphere.

Among the ten thousand pieces of correspondence the bishops are said to have received—all of which, we are told, they read—was a brief letter I wrote after having vainly attempted to interest more visible and powerful leaders within the disabled community in communicating with the bishops. (One might surmise that people with disabilites have begun to discount the effectiveness of the Church's leadership and have gone elsewhere to seek their rights.)

In my letter I merely requested that some attention be directed to the unacceptable levels of unemployment among the disabled. I pointed out that most disabled workers are in fact exempt from the minimum-wage law, which is itself hardly adequate to ensure a decent family life or even a decent existence as a single adult. I wrote that I could only surmise that the bishops' concern for the disabled was lumped into the section emphasizing the hardships of the countless poor throughout this land of plenty. Such lumping together, I suggested, would have the added effect of keeping persons with disabilities invisible, and as invisible, too easily overlooked.

PAPAL STATEMENTS ON THE HANDICAPPED

Lest we lose heart totally, we must acknowledge that Pope John Paul II has specifically focused on the disabled in several documents, as well as in his travels throughout the world. In the spring of 1981, addressing a congress of the National Association of Crippled and Disabled Persons of Work, the pope very clearly praised their success in achieving its members' "reintegration into social life, saving them from loneliness and moral discouragement, starting them along the way to a necessary human relationship" (#1). He insisted "that every person—but in particular those most exposed to exclusion because of their precarious health conditions—must be guaranteed his inalienable dignity, human, social, and spiritual" (#2). Every individual suffering on account of any handicap, he said, should be helped to "become aware of his dignity and his values and to realize that something is expected of him and that he, too, can and must contribute to the progress and good of the family and its community" (#3).

Again, during his Canadian pilgrimage in the fall of 1984, Pope John Paul II spoke to a disabled audience at the François-Charon Rehabilitation Center in Quebec and reaffirmed, in unequivocal terms, disabled persons' entitlement to the full dignity of the human condition:

> The handicapped person is a human subject in the full sense, with all the innate, sacred and inviolable rights that entails. This is true whether the person be handicapped by physical disability, whether due to birth defects, chronic disease or accident, or by mental or sensory deficiency. It is true, too, no matter how great the person's affliction might be. We must facilitate his or her participation in all facets of social life and at all possible levels: in the family, at school, at work, in the community, in politics and religion (#3).

We can only be gratified by the pope's clear-cut and specific incorporation of the disabled into that human community to which the full privileges of human dignity must be extended.

Pope John Paul II has always reached out to the disabled. I can myself recall waiting with my family for hours, in freezing temperatures, during his first papal visit to Chicago. There was a group of disabled persons also waiting, and one could feel his warm response to this group waiting for his acknowledgment. During the summer of 1987, in St. Peter's Square in Rome, I again experienced John Paul II's enthusiastic reaching out to greet and touch disabled members of a huge public audience. And during his most recent trip to the United States, newspapers, magazines, and television showed the pope crossing the auditorium after Mass to embrace and kiss the young armless guitar player.

These outpourings of warmth and recognition must not be minimized. There is obvious sincerity in these gestures, but we would be derelict if we were satisfied with this level of recognition and came to think that human rights and human dignity had been achieved.

We must also note how quickly in John Paul II's 1984 address in Quebec he passed beyond the expression of concern for disabled persons to the well-deserved commendation of those who assist them in their need. One cannot help being reminded of an all-too-common phenomenon, of people who seem unable to address disabled persons directly but instead refer inquiries to attendants, onlookers, bystanders—to anyone except the human person with disabilities who stands before them.

And one cannot help recalling the words of the *Pastoral Statement on Persons with Disabilities:* "what disabled individuals need, first of all, is acceptance in this difference that can neither be denied nor overlooked" (#3).

Nevertheless, we must concede that a new note has been sounded and that today we no longer have to assume the inclusion of disabled individuals. The Church's public statements clearly acknowledge their existence. The task now is to turn our words, excellent though they be, into action, if we are ever really to include the disabled.

THE HANDICAPPED IN MINISTRY

In perhaps the most exciting passage of the *Pastoral Statement on Persons with Disabilities,* the American bishops wrote that they "applaud recent decisions to accept qualified candidates for ordination or the religious life in spite of their significant disabilities" (#24). This is astounding news, long overdue. I myself remember that I, when but a girl eager to join a convent, waited many months for a supportive bishop to locate one that would accept a blind postulant. He eventually found one but informed me that my request had been very difficult to fulfill.

Celebrate and Challenge, published in 1988 upon the tenth anniversary of the *Pastoral Statement of U.S. Catholic Bishops on Persons with Disabilities,* welcomed and even encouraged disabled candidates for ordination and service at that altar so long out of bounds to them:

> We proclaim that if any disabled person is prevented from active participation, the Church community is incomplete. We call upon Church leadership throughout the country to encourage conversion of mind and heart, so that all persons with disabilities may be invited to worship and to every level of service as full members of the body of Christ.

It remains, at least, an option, and a direct counter to the offensive proscriptions of Leviticus.

But the ancient proscription of Leviticus had not been universally observed anyway—for which we offer thanks and praise to God. Some orders and some churches have welcomed persons with physical disabilities and allowed them to serve as ministers. Truly, such openness is a reflection of the kingdom of God manifesting itself in our midst.

I have been privileged to know a former priest of the Augustinian order, an intelligent man, kind and wise, who brought joy and God's presence wherever he went. He was a living witness to the wisdom that—long before any change in canon law—had not refused him admission to the priesthood because of severe scoliosis of the spine. The other priests of his order had welcomed him and enabled him to function in their community for many years. Despite significant disfigurement, his superiors had not turned away from "that wall of strangeness" but had accepted him in that "difference that can neither be denied nor overlooked."

The United Church of Christ dedicated Access Sunday, the first Sunday of October, 1995, to individuals with various types of disabilities. At Peoples' Church in Chicago, Nancy Nyberg, a woman disabled by multiple sclerosis, delivered the homily. In her remarks she included gay and lesbian people who have been publicly excluded from participation in many a Christian church. And she was clear in stating that her experience as an ordained minister of the gospel message led her to observe that the most prejudiced, unaccepting people are too frequently those who think of themselves as good Christians.

Lest the full import of their various public statements lose vigor and falter on the way to implementation, the Catholic bishops published *Guidelines for the Celebration of the Sacraments with Persons with Disabilities* on June 16, 1995.

The bishops began by reviewing their previous documents. They recalled that in their pastoral statements published in 1978 and 1988 they had called for broader integration of persons with disabilities into the full life of the Church through increased evangelization, catechesis, and participation in the Church's sacramental life.

The *Guidelines* affirmed and clarified these previous statements and, further, advocated ministry by persons with disabilities. First setting forth general principles, it then proceeded through each of the sacraments: baptism, confirmation, Eucharist, reconciliation, anointing of the sick, marriage, and holy orders, offering clarification and some detail as to how persons with disabilities might most fully participate in the life of the Church.

One might consider these three statements as a triptych: three self-contained units forming one integrated whole. In a sense, these three statements are a trinity in which persons with disabilities may more clearly come to understand their rightful position in the Church, which is essentially one body comprised of many parts.

The *Pastoral Statement on Persons with Disabilities* had declared that "to exclude any member of the parish from these celebrations of the life of the church, even by passive omission, is to deny the reality of that community" (#23). The *Guidelines* further stated that true accessibility involves far more than physical alterations of buildings and programs. However, the bishops clearly realized that cooperation in accessibility is a two-way street. Persons with disabilities must not avoid searching for appropriate strategies of accessibility through responsible requests and appropriate involvement.

On April 22, 1996 the Chicago Church witnessed how this type of inclusion might harmoniously come about when its archbishop, Joseph Cardinal Bernardin, gathered persons with disabilities and those interested in their inclusion into a celebration of the liturgy. This first-ever conference of disabled persons, "That All May Worship," was convened at St. Monica's Church. There, in this totally accessible environment, more than seven hundred persons witnessed the solemnity of total inclusion as we worshiped together. The ministers represented a variety of persons with disabilities, participating respectfully with others and announcing to all present and to all who would read of this event that the kingdom of God is truly visible from time to time in our very midst.

THE LUTHERAN EXPERIENCE

Other religious institutions have also reexamined their commitment to disabled members of their communities, not always with total success. Nancy L. Eiesland, in her book *The Disabled God,* recounts that in 1980 the General Convention of the American Lutheran Church (ALC) adopted a resolution concerning ministry by persons with disabilities. The resolution was designed to prepare the ALC for the observance of the United Nations International Year of the Disabled in 1981.

Included in the resolution was a theological statement entitled "The Church and Persons with Handicaps: Unmasking a Hidden Curriculum of the Christian Community"; a supplementary section entitled "Issues and Implications Evolving from the Theological Statement"; and a church-school curriculum titled "An ABC Primer of Faith for the Children of Access." The General Convention ratified the following recommendations:

1. That the divisions and service boards of the ALC, as well as related agencies and institutions, should examine the implications of this statement for their work and reflect the concerns it incorporates;
2. That the ALC should promote the United Nations International Year of the Disabled;
3. That every district of the ALC be encouraged to implement the concerns embodied in this resolution; and
4. That the ALC's office of Communication and Mission Support should study the feasibility of developing programs to address the attitudinal, architectural, and communication barriers that prevent full access by persons with disabilities (#58).

The General Convention of the ALC wholeheartedly embraced the concerns of persons with disabilities and encouraged systemic change. Yet just five years after the unanimous ratification of this resolution, the council of the ALC announced at its 1986 General Convention that people with "significant" physical or mental handicaps should be barred from ordained ministry in the denomination. What had happened?

Despite its broad and well-intentioned goals, the ALC's theology of access and resolution was a nonstarter. The institutional change it enjoined did not occur; the issues and implications it raised were affirmed as morally and socially laudable but never satisfactorily incorporated into its practices. And the local education it proposed was not adequately implemented. The denomination that had previously stated that the "wholeness of the family of God demands not only compassion for the disabled but also their inclusion as fully committed members of the body of Christ who are able to witness and minister" (#17), now asserted that "pastors are expected to be sufficiently able-bodied, ambulatory and mobile to carry out normal parish duties" (#8). Particularly excluded from ministry were persons with neurological disorders such as multiple sclerosis and impairments such as quadriplegia (#75–76).

We must all recognize that some physical conditions may well render an individual incapable of this or that particular function, but shouldn't we avoid a blanket rejection of all individuals with disabilities, regardless of individual situations?

In 1983 the Levitical proscriptions were discreetly dropped from the Roman Catholic Code of Canon Law, but no positive statements of inclusion were inserted. The result was something analogous to a black hole—a void that needed to be filled. In the bishops' *Pastoral Statement on Persons with Disabilities* we found at last a positive affirmation that the disabled are indeed qualified to serve God's people and to serve at God's altar in the Roman Catholic tradition of worship.

We must now watch and pray that a backlash similar to that of the ALC does not occur in reaction against this laudable statement of the American bishops, and that the Church does not follow the example of backlash occurring in the secular sphere as the Americans with Disabilities Act comes under increased attack.

7

EXPERIENCING THE KINGDOM

Jesus often told his followers that "...the kingdom of God is among you" (Luke 11:20, 17:21). As modern would-be followers of Jesus, we are quick to proclaim that we believe what he said. Yet our actions indicate that we consider the kingdom of God in our midst as one of those rhetorical devices good preachers frequently use to capture the attention of their listeners.

Jesus was a good preacher. He often used metaphor and hyperbole, analogy and parable, to explain something important, something he wanted his followers to remember. Sometimes Jesus would answer questions by telling his followers stories, in true rabbinical tradition, the better to illustrate the point in question. So where is this kingdom of God he spoke of as being in our midst? Where can it be found, and where and when can we experience it? What will this experience mean when it happens? We are eager to experience the kingdom, but we are not sure where to search.

In *A Rumor of Angels,* Peter Berger laments our inability to recognize the signposts all about us that point us beyond our earthly existence to what lies beyond, to the transcendent reality of God's immense concern for all creation, to the kingdom of God in our very midst. We believe all that Jesus told us, and we know that "...faith is the assurance of things hoped for, the conviction of things not seen" (Hebrews 11:1).

We believe this, but as creatures of the here and now we must discover concrete examples to anchor our drifting beliefs and harbor us in certitude lest we go astray on the way. But we must realize that this inability to recognize the signals of the transcendent is not exclusively characteristic of our modern age.

On the road to Emmaus, after Jesus' crucifixion and Resurrection, Jesus encountered two of his own disciples who were incapable of remarking the transcendent alive in their very midst. As Luke narrated,

> While they were talking and discussing, Jesus himself came near and went with them, but their eyes were kept from recognizing him. And he said to them, "What are you discussing with each other while you walk along?" They stood still, looking sad. Then one of them, whose name was Cleopas, answered him, "Are you the only stranger in Jerusalem who does not know the things that have taken place there in these days?" He asked them, "What things?" (Luke 24:15–19).

As they continued along the road, Jesus resumed his former role of teacher, expounding the messages of Moses and the prophets. As they approached the village to which they were going, he gave the impression that he was going on farther. But they urged him, "'Stay with us, because it is almost evening and the day is now nearly over'" (24:29).

By inviting the stranger in to share their meal, the two disciples ceased to be strangers and became companions with Jesus. Then, "when he was at the table with them, he took bread, blessed and broke it, and gave it to them. Then their eyes were opened, and they recognized him; and he vanished from their sight" (24:30–31). The two disciples knew him in the breaking of the bread, as we come to know the stranger on our road by sharing our bread with him or her. As Jesus' disciples, we too often fail to recognize the stranger, to open our eyes to the signals of the transcendent all about us.

Let us begin looking for evidence that the kingdom of God is in our very midst. Let us attempt to discern how the signals all around us may be pointers to the transcendent.

A PARABLE FOR MINISTERS WORKING IN THE FIELD

Once a lay minister, working for and with persons with disabilities, came to Jesus and asked, "Lord, how may I experience the kingdom of God here on earth as I work with and for your people with disabilities?"

And Jesus looked upon this modern disciple with love and said, "Love God with all your heart, and treat your neighbor as yourself, and then you will begin to perceive the outlines of the kingdom of God emerging visibly in your midst."

But the person wished to clarify this answer and so asked, "And who is my neighbor, Lord?"

Jesus replied, "Once there was a simple woman who grieved deeply with her good husband when their firstborn child arrived, mentally deficient according to medical and social understanding. They accepted the child, welcoming this new arrival into our troubled world, and began caring for and loving their small, wounded son.

"Eventually, with their love and care, the tiny baby grew up physically, but he did not increase in wisdom and intelligence as his small body grew. The woman, wishing to provide every good experience for her little son, began to teach him meaningful things, including the latest enthusiasm in urban sports: rollerblading along the expanse of Lake Michigan that borders their great city, Chicago.

"One day people saw this little boy and his mother, properly protected with helmets and pads, joyfully making their precarious way along the Drive on shiny new roller blades— some onlookers inwardly wondering, no doubt, why such a child should even have been allowed to come to term in our modern day of medical expediency.

"Such people looked on them with pity. God's kingdom was hidden from their eyes as surely as it was hidden from the eyes of the two disciples on the road to Emmaus.

"Other people, perhaps with secret difficulties of their own, were able to realize that this little child and his young mother were bringing hope and understanding into the darkened souls of the onlookers who smiled at the sight, and who were beginning to discern the kingdom of God in their midst."

The lay minister thanked Jesus and began to reflect on this story.

Then Jesus began telling another story:

"A young couple had wanted a child for a very long time and had finally decided to adopt one since they had none of their own. All the plans were made, and they eagerly awaited the day when a new baby would be available for them to take into their own family. Not long after their request for adoption, they received a phone call announcing that a newborn baby was available for adoption, but there was a medical problem due to the mother's being prescribed thalidomide during pregnancy.

"They pondered over this difficult news and asked God for guidance in a very difficult decision. What might this medical problem be? The hospital had told them that they would not be informed of specific disabilities until they had made up their minds one way or the other. 'Well,' the woman said to her husband, 'if this were our own flesh and blood, what would we do?' So the decision was made, and they accepted a little girl who had been born with only one leg.

"Friends and relations were amazed, even shocked, at their decision, but the couple rejoiced and delighted in the little girl and eagerly set about the work of building a home for the new member of their family. When she had grown a little, the couple adopted a little boy to complete their family. Thus does the kingdom of God come into our midst."

And Jesus might have turned to his listeners and asked, "Do you understand what I am saying to you?"

Another time, Jesus said, ""...seeing they do not perceive, and hearing they do not listen, nor do they understand""" (Matthew 13:13). One of Jesus' listeners asked him what he meant by this statement, and Jesus began telling her a story:

"Once there was a man who walked proudly on his way, greeting neighbors and welcoming strangers as he strode confidently through the world. He was a good man with good, caring intentions and hoped that by his example others would behave well.

"Oftentimes as he walked along the streets of his neighborhood, he would spy the familiar figure of a blind woman on her way to a meeting or to the store. With a smile on his lips and the best of intentions in his heart, he would step forward. 'You know,' he would say to anyone who would listen, as the blind woman drew nearer, 'blind people have extrasensitive hearing and are able to identify any voices they have heard before. They know precisely who is speaking to them. It is truly a gift from God.'

"With that he would go up to the blind woman and say, in a loud voice so that she as well as all the onlookers might better hear him, 'I know you know who this is? Don't you?' Of course she knew, for he frequently played this embarrassing game. She would quickly but quietly respond, attempting to overcome her awkwardness at this patronizing, humiliating treatment, inwardly hoping their paths would not cross again.

"That man, certain that he was free of prejudice, was more intent on his own self-righteousness, his own image in the eyes of those who could watch him, than on the humble acknowledgment that his was only one small—and intrusive—voice in a blind woman's world full of voices. If he had considered the situation from her point of view, or from any perspective besides his own—if he had known anything about what the kingdom of God among us means—he would have known that all that was needed was for him to have quietly mentioned his name while offering her a warm greeting."

This story provides an example of the many misperceptions and much ignorance there are about the disabled. Many well-intentioned, temporarily able bodied people believe that when one physical sense is lacking, other senses make up for the deprivation. Not so! It is true that people who have limited vision, or no sight at all, seem to have better hearing, but that is simply because they have to pay attention very closely to the sounds around them, whereas a sighted person simply needs to glance around to survey the surroundings.

Another example is the widespread belief that guide dogs can read traffic lights and thus safely guide their masters or mistresses across busy streets. The truth is that dogs, as well as persons with little or no sight, are color blind, and the blind person is simply paying close attention to the sound of traffic to determine when it is safe to cross. So if no traffic was heard, and the light was against crossing the street, the blind person, with or without a dog, would simply go ahead, despite the warning of the traffic signal. Such misperceptions become stereotypes, and these are harmful because they establish false expectations, prejudices, and fears that are almost impossible to remove. They prevent us from treating the disabled individual in front of us as a fellow human being, from showing him or her the love due to all God's children.

One time when Jesus was surrounded by little children, he told his disciples and all who were standing about, "'If any of you put a stumbling block before one of these little ones who believe in me, it would be better for you if a great millstone were fastened around your neck and you were drowned in the depth of the sea'" (Matthew 18:6). Knowing that children place all their trust in their parents and other adults, Jesus was warning his disciples not to teach their own stereotypes to children—not to scandalize, thwart, or twist a young child's perceptions with harmful and erroneous information about people who are different. Children understand people openly, as they are, unless grownups have already imposed prejudices on them.

As a blind mother I often had occasion to guard against unknowingly influencing my children's trust in my capabilities. One day after I had sent my older children off to school, I decided to take a walk with my two youngest boys. The older one was about four years old, and his younger brother about two. We put on our jackets and headed out for the morning's adventure. The day was lovely, and the sun was warm as we left the house. "You take one of Paul's hands, Christopher," I told the older boy, "and I'll take the other. Here we go."

As we approached a quiet side street in our neighborhood I paused, listening for any traffic, and Christopher said, "You listen, Mom, and I watch, and we'll get across OK."

I had never discussed the procedures and precautions of our morning stroll. My children simply expected that I knew where I was going and that by following my direction, all would be well.

It is vital that parents realize that children at a very early age begin imitating the actions, words, and attitudes they have observed. If grownups consciously or unconsciously react negatively to people who are different, they may easily scandalize these little ones. Staring or glaring at a disabled person or reviling a particular handicap will teach children, more effectively than deliberate lectures, that people with disabilites are somehow outcast.

Of course, the disabled can do a great work in showing others the way to the kingdom of God. Unfortunately, people with disabilities are themselves not always free from prejudice toward people who are different from them, even toward those who might have different disabilities.

REMOVE THE BEAM IN YOUR OWN EYE
(LUKE 6:41–42)

I became acutely aware of prejudice among the disabled— the so-called hierarchy of disabilities—when I worked in the Center for Program Development and the Handicapped for Chicago's City-Wide College, largely staffed by persons with every sort of disability.

At first I tended to avoid certain co-workers, and I sensed that I also was being avoided. Perhaps we were embarrassed, or perhaps we were trying to determine how we might relate to one another. It was extremely awkward until, one day, one of the typists, a young woman in a wheelchair, asked me if I would go shopping at Marshall Fields with her during lunch. She said that she needed help in the music department. It was down a flight of stairs, and her wheelchair could not get her there.

We went along, she in her wheelchair alongside the curb of the busy downtown street, and I along the sidewalk with my guide dog. At Marshall Fields she mentioned that she also wanted to buy her sister a blouse for her birthday but knew that she could not reach the racks to pick one out. It was simple. I took blouses down for her, and she read the price tags. Then we went off to the music department to buy the latest pop recordings, and she waited for me to descend the stairs and return with the various albums she wanted. We worked well together: she read the albums, I navigated the stairs, and the wall between at least two employees began to fall.

Back in the office, we began cooperating to achieve what we needed: she would read to me, and I would get things off shelves that she could not reach by herself. It was a good system, and one that gently began revealing the kingdom of God to us.

This mutual acceptance did not come about spontaneously, but when it did occur, it was a rich reward well worth the effort. Is not this a glimpse of God's kingdom? Is not this what Jesus meant when he told his followers that the kingdom of God was in their very midst?

Prejudice seems part of the human condition. But as we all—the disabled and temporarily abled alike—make efforts to work together, there will be many opportunities to understand and accept one another as we are.

Two Men Went Up to the Temple to Pray
(Luke 18:10–14)

Remember the familiar story Jesus once told about the two men who went up to the temple to pray? One was a Pharisee, the other a publican. The Pharisee prayed, "Thank God that I am not a sinner like this publican." Meanwhile, the publican, with head bowed, simply asked God to forgive him because he was a sinner.

Well, the following story is my variation on this important theme:

One morning, two men were on their way to an early-morning healing liturgy for disabled and sick parishioners. One man was a permanent deacon; the other, an investigator for the IRS. Both were members of the parish, wishing to participate in this very moving ritual, which was to include the anointing of the sick.

Entering the church, they saw a priest with a few women acting as assistants. And they also saw wheelchairs and walkers, various types of canes and crutches, and the full assortment of the aids persons with disabilities require. There were worried-looking parents holding the hands of obviously mentally retarded children, children who seemed happily unaware of the important occasion.

On one side of the aisle there were several young men, emaciated and horribly weakened by AIDS. The deacon reflected on the previous Sunday's reading from Luke's Gospel, in which Jesus healed the ten lepers. These men with AIDS, certainly, were modern lepers, living in our very midst.

Avoiding that side of the aisle, he looked about and inwardly thanked God that he was not as any of these. *I have no need of a wheelchair, a walker, or a white cane. I care for my body,* he said to himself. *I take good care of my eyes and make sure I have a thorough physical every six months.* Turning his attention to the young men hideously emaciated and weakened by AIDS, he thought, *I live by God's law and do not contaminate my body and soul as these poor young men have obviously done. Thank you, Lord, for you have carefully guided me along righteous paths.*

With that, ready to assume his important role as deacon, he made his way to the altar and offered his services to the priest and the servers who were vesting for the anointing. With such a throng, his services were in great need.

But the IRS investigator, standing in the rear of the church, was so overwhelmed with the sight that he bowed down his head and prayed that somehow he might be able to help, to encourage, to befriend these people. *Perhaps, Lord, I might offer several of them a ride home. Perhaps that blind man over there needs someone to read to him. What about that lady in the wheelchair, Lord? Perhaps I could help her with her shopping or drive her to a movie or a concert?*

He could hardly raise his head as he prayed, but he knew that when the anointing was over, he would wait outside to see if anybody needed his help, and then leave his name and address and phone number at the rectory just in case he might be needed.

He noticed the pale young men with AIDS. *Perhaps they might need me to visit them or to invite them to my home,* he thought. And with that he made his way across the aisle and sat with them, asking if anyone needed a ride.

Jesus might well have remarked, "This man went home justified, but the other did not."

ANOTHER GOOD SAMARITAN
(LUKE 10:29–37)

Once upon a time, in a big city, there was a blind man who often walked in the neighborhood with his fine looking dog-guide, a yellow Labrador. People would admire his fine dog as they passed by him on their way to work, school, and church. Often they would comment to one another how smart the dog was and wondered if they could help the man in any way. But nobody ever approached the man to be a neighbor to him.

After several years passed, one of the activist parishioners took it upon herself to approach the man after Mass and offer assistance. Arriving in front of the blind man's pew, she opened the conversation by asking, "Who takes your guide dog out?"

Surprised, the man replied, "Why, I do," wondering why such a question should be asked after so many years in the parish.

If she had really wanted to offer assistance, and had asked the blind man what he might need, perhaps he might have asked about meetings, about parish or local events, about various liturgies or other things important to a member of a parish community. People assume too many things about persons with disabilities and take it upon themselves to offer unneeded and even offensive assistance in lieu of offering a friendship or asking questions that might more normally lead to appropriate help or useful information.

In my own parish, though I had lived and worshiped there for several years, I was never made aware of the availability of receiving the Eucharist in both species until a visiting mission priest followed me out of the church one morning and asked if I would like to partake of the chalice as everyone else who wished to had. Not having known until that moment that this was available, I was very pleased and quickly said, "Of course. Thank you very much." And inwardly I wondered what else I might be missing.

People with sight limitations do not have access to church bulletins, newspapers, and other sorts of printed information. A hot line to the rectory or to the home of someone who would provide information about meetings and events could be just the type of contact many persons now lack, to the effect that they feel like strangers and outsiders in their own church and community.

Such a hot line would not be as costly as architectural structures might be, but it would be invaluable. One of the members of the parish, perhaps one disabled in some way, might eagerly serve as such a channel of information and thereby become an important member of the parish community.

PICKING YOUR OWN DISABILITY

A familiar story that turns up on retreats or days of recollection is the one about a person who complained about the cross she had to bear. "It's too heavy! Why so much suffering for me? I have enough!" And so on the complaints went until Jesus, in a dream or vision, said he would give that person a choice.

Up to the great eternal hall she was taken and shown a variety of crosses: big ones, little ones, heavy ones, lighter ones. Finally, she made her selection. "This one will do," she told Jesus, and as she left lugging her cross—for we all have crosses to bear—Jesus noted that she had selected as easiest to bear the very one of which she had been complaining.

Have you ever thought what disability you would pick if you had to have one and were given the opportunity to choose? What limitation do you think you could most readily embrace and learn to live and work with?

Some organizations set aside a day to simulate how it would feel to be handicapped. They provide a variety of props: wheelchairs, blindfolds, canes, ear plugs, and all sorts of devices through which volunteers may plunge into the unknown world of disability. (Blindness, incidentally, holds the dubious distinction of being the cross least chosen, most feared, and also most misunderstood.) The goal is that these people will then know what it is like to be disabled. Some few persons might comprehend, a little, how confining it is to be in a wheelchair, or to depend on crutches or even a walker, but none will gain anything approaching full comprehension of having no alternative. This exercise is not a good means of seriously understanding the position of a person who did not select a particular disability.

Those who find themselves with a disability must begin to work their way into living with alternative skills, training, education. This comes about only after inner acceptance and spiritual healing have begun. Only then can these people too begin to share their many capabilities in whatever environment they find themselves.

STEREOTYPES DIE HARD

A close relative phoned me one night to share an experience she felt gave her significant insight into my situation. She was in the washroom at a shopping center when all the lights suddenly went out. She confided, "I was in there by myself, and I couldn't find anything at all. I thought of you and began to wonder how you are able to locate things when you are all alone with nobody about to show you."

I tried to explain to her—probably not too successfully, for stereotypes die hard—that I had had quite a few years to experiment with getting around a washroom. Certainly, to compare my experience with someone who has just lost all sight, or with someone who simply finds herself temporarily in the dark, is scarcely appropriate. People with physical impairments must learn alternate techniques, alternative means of dealing with almost every situation. To attempt to explain each particular tactic would be pointless; rather, the overall training and skill comes about with acceptance, education, training, and experience.

IN THE EYE OF THE BEHOLDER

Once in a college where I was teaching an amateur film buff came and asked if I would participate in a short film he hoped might win a prize in a local short-movie competition he had entered. The concept was simple: he gathered together an assortment of people with a variety of disabilities—visual, physical, and auditory—around a library table. We were all simply talking as he shot endless footage of our intense conversation.

Later, as I watched the completed product with a friend, he described how it opened by simply showing this group of rather good looking young people in animated conversation. But as the camera drew back from its primary focus, other things came into view: a wheelchair, a guide dog, a wire from a hearing aid, the truncated body of a man who had been born after his mother had taken thalidomide during pregnancy.

And now "the wall of strangeness" of which the bishops wrote in their *Pastoral Statement on Persons with Disabilities* was erected once more. Up until that final shot, we were an ordinary group of people engrossed in a discussion of current events or a criticism of significant literary works—intelligent, articulate people engaged in a serious conversation. The impact, according to my friend—someone free of any strangeness—was most effective.

I began to think of possible titles for this film: *Talking Heads.* That's been used. *There's More Here Than Meets the Eye.* I liked that one. At the time I thought maybe he'd use it. I don't think he did. Did the film win? No, but the message was clear and deeply significant for those who had the chance to view it.

I Have Set Before You Life and Death. Choose Life!
(Deuteronomy 30:19)

In his recent autobiography, *A Moving Violation* (1995), John Hockenberry, a rather well-known reporter for National Public Radio, relates numerous anecdotes about his attempts to put his life back into perspective after being paralyzed in an auto accident when he was a college student. He underwent rehabilitation, learned all sorts of helpful, vital alternate techniques, and obtained an established position in a physically as well as emotionally demanding profession, covering many overseas and wartime assignments.

He tells also of his shock when once a flight attendant, making her way down the aisle of the airplane with drinks, stopped alongside him and casually asked, as she offered him a drink and a little bag of peanuts, why he hadn't committed suicide yet.

Stunned by her question, he paused, considered for a moment, and asked for his snack.

But she continued, concerned for his sexual prowess, "Can you still do it?"

Startled, now annoyed, he once more turned her attention to his cola and bag of peanuts.

More bumptious than most, this outspoken young woman was simply voicing the public's general curiosity about people with disabilities. Amazing as it seems when written out for all to see, the message is clear: it is better to be dead than to accept whatever seems to the viewer to be unacceptable. Better to choose death than life.

I know of others with disabilities who have heard complete strangers whisper, "I'd rather be dead than like that!" as they walked by.

One afternoon as I was returning from lunch in a downtown restaurant near the office where I worked for the Federal Department of Education, I heard a man begging passersby for money to get something to eat. I heard footsteps pass him quickly by and felt discouraged at the indifference of the public. Reaching into my purse, I turned about to face the man, having listened to the direction of his voice of supplication, and offered a single dollar bill as I said, "I hope this will help a little."

He paused. I waited. As he turned away I heard him say to the people as they pushed past him, "I'm not that bad off yet!" He walked away as I stood, dollar in hand. I suppose he too would rather have been dead than like that.

We began this chapter by referring to Berger's *A Rumor of*

Angels, lamenting our inability to remark signposts of the transcendent in our midst. If we could only see them, they would point us past the here and now to something beyond our journey, beyond our finite difficulties, beyond our and others' disabilities—even beyond the crucifixion. And it would become clear, as Dietrich Bonhoeffer wrote, that "all historical events are 'penultimate,' that their ultimate significance lies in a reality that transcends them..." (Berger 181).

We find ourselves back on the road to Emmaus. The stranger has vanished, and our hearts are burning within us because we failed to recognize him in the little child born with one leg, or the young man with his body emaciated and weakened by AIDS, or the blind man, or the woman in the wheelchair. Not until we become aware of the signs of the transcendent all about us—not until we recognize these strangers as companions on our own road to Emmaus—will we recognize Jesus and be able to discern the kingdom of God alive in our very midst.

8

A NEW CREATION: MINISTERING IN A CHURCH WITHOUT BARRIERS

A nd how shall all these things be accomplished? How shall we bring about a metanoia, a changing of attitudes, creating hearts of flesh where once there were hearts of stone?

Paul Tillich speaks of a "manifestation of a new creation" here and there and now and then, even within ourselves. This new creation, in its many guises, is the kingdom of which Jesus spoke. It is not announced with neon signs but hidden, awaiting our discovery as the veils of doubt and distrust begin dropping like scales from our eyes.

"There is nothing new under the sun," King Solomon wisely said, and we agree. Yet we finite beings forget these sage words and continuously reinvent, re-create that which has existed for centuries.

Two thousand years ago Saint Paul left us the model for ministry in a church without barriers when he wrote to the Galatians, "There is no longer Jew or Greek, there is no longer slave or free, there is no longer male and female; for all of you are one in Christ Jesus" (3:28). Are these words not evidence of what we moderns call "a theology of inclusion"?

And in Paul's letters to the Corinthians, we discover something remarkably modern, something remarkably like liberation theology, which we have thought came to life only in the past thirty years. Paul wrote about the variety of talents within the body of the Church, the many various gifts we possess:

> Now concerning spiritual gifts, brothers and sisters, I do not want you to be uninformed....Now there are varieties of gifts, but the same Spirit; and there are varieties of services, but the same Lord; and there are varieties of activities, but it is the same God who activates all of them in everyone. To each is given the manifestation of the Spirit for the common good. To one is given through the Spirit the utterance of wisdom, and to another the utterance of knowledge according to the same Spirit, to another faith by the same Spirit, to another gifts of healing by the one Spirit, to another the working of miracles, to another prophecy, to another the discernment of spirits, to another various kinds of tongues, to another the interpretation of tongues. All these are activated by one and the same Spirit, who allots to each one individually just as the Spirit chooses (1 Corinthians 12:1–11).

And when Paul continued regarding the Mystical Body, was he not directly addressing us today as we ponder how persons with disabilities can become ministers of the Church? We ask, "But *what* can they do?"

Paul wrote,

> For just as the body is one and has many members, and all the members of the body, though many, are one body, so it is with Christ. For in the one Spirit we were all baptized into one body—Jews or Greeks, slaves or free—and we were all made to drink of one Spirit.
>
> Indeed, the body does not consist of one member but of many. If the foot would say, "Because I am not a hand, I do not belong to the body," that would not make it any less a

part of the body. And if the ear would say, "Because I am not an eye, I do not belong to the body," that would not make it any less a part of the body. If the whole body were an eye, where would the hearing be? If the whole body were hearing, where would the sense of smell be? But as it is, God arranged the members in the body, each one of them, as he chose. If all were a single member, where would the body be? As it is, there are many members, yet one body. The eye cannot say to the hand, "I have no need of you," nor again the head to the feet, "I have no need of you." On the contrary, the members of the body that seem to be weaker are indispensable, and those members of the body that we think less honorable we clothe with greater honor, and our less respectable members are treated with greater respect; whereas our more respectable members do not need this. But God has so arranged the body, giving the greater honor to the inferior member, that there may be no dissension within the body, but the members may have the same care for one another. If one member suffers, all suffer together with it; if one member is honored, all rejoice together with it.

Now you are the body of Christ and individually members of it. And God has appointed in the church first apostles, second prophets, third teachers; then deeds of power, then gifts of healing, forms of assistance, forms of leadership, various kinds of tongues. Are all apostles? Are all prophets? Are all teachers? Do all work miracles? Do all possess gifts of healing? Do all speak in tongues? Do all interpret? But strive for the greater gifts (1 Corinthians 12:12–31).

These words have become too familiar. We might even be able to repeat them from memory. We would do well to read them again, pondering their meaning in Saint Paul's day and in ours, to recover a sense of their rich significance.

Fortunately, there are signs that the modern Church has not completely overlooked these words. For example, the Priests' Senate of the Chicago Archdiocese requested that persons involved in ministry for and with persons with disabilities address a conference of priests, to present their concerns in person.

A committee comprised of persons with disabilities had been formed early in 1990 to assist a graduate student from the Catholic Theological Union in her survey of the accessibility of our local churches. This committee had established a speakers' bureau, and three members of this bureau were eager to respond to the priests' invitation: an attractive businesswoman, born deaf, who is an active member of the Cathedral Parish of the archdiocese; a severely mobility impaired woman in a wheelchair, mother of several children, wife of a permanent deacon, and herself a reader and homilist in her parish; and I, at that time a teacher in the college seminary, a wife, and mother of five grown children, blind since the age of ten.

I have since come to consider that meeting one of those penultimate events signaling that the kingdom is alive! The following is my part of the presentation offered on that occasion:

"Words, words, words!" This was Hamlet's response to Polonius.

"And what is the matter, my lord?"

The matter is simply that there have been too many words of late. Laws passed, proclamations made, attempting to deal with, shall we say, "the handicapped question," "the handicapped solution."

After one hundred years of social documents in which little or nothing has been said of the plight of disabled individuals, John Paul II has specifically addressed the Church's concern for disabled individuals. And now the bishops' letter moves toward making his words a reality.

These are all good words, giving us hope, but they are only words, and they are as dead as the dry bones in the book of the prophet Ezekiel, waiting for life, for spirit to be breathed into them, these dead bones, to bring them to life, to enable them to rise up and walk about like the Mystical Body of Christ—to walk about and do the work of God in our communities.

If the work is not done, it is not God who has failed, but our own hands that have kept God from reaching out, and our own feet that have kept God from walking to those in need. We are God's body, and by our actions God works in the world or does not work in the world.

So the question we asked at the outset of all of this is still What is the matter?

The matter is precisely what we are about today.

What do we seek?

We seek "acceptance in our differences, which can neither be denied nor overlooked."

What do we want?

We want full membership in the community of the Church. We want a chance to share our talents and our gifts—of which we have many. They have been given us by God, and we ask to share them with the rest of the community of believers.

What can we do?

Ask us. Many things. All sorts of things. There is nothing we or someone among us cannot do. Of course, for persons who are visually impaired, my own particular condition, driving the school bus might be problematic.

What have we done? Ask us. Many things:

One friend of mine has worked in the soup kitchen at his church. Another friend has been a lector, reader, welcomed at St. Joseph's and St. Andrew's. Another visually impaired woman has been teaching CCD classes. Yet I also know several visually impaired persons who have not been welcomed by their parish leaders, who have been discouraged from seeking active roles. That "strangeness" to which the bishops refer could not be overcome. (We note, as an aside, that as the formation of an office "for the disabled" was going forward, nobody with a disability was invited to join this effort. It was priests only!)

Two of us have been studying theology at the Catholic Theological Union (CTU), the largest graduate seminary in the United States, earning degrees in theology in hopes of being more useful to our Church by increasing our understanding of its doctrines. As I have mentioned, I myself was a professor at the archdiocesan seminary, Niles College, until 1989, teaching English, philosophy, and a little theology on the side.

Just this past year two disabled friends of mine have challenged the stereotype—have, in the latest jargon, pushed the envelope—and I must share their achievements with you:

A young doctoral candidate at the University of Illinois, blind since birth, went on a world pilgrimage walk for peace. He traversed thousands of miles, bearing his white cane as his pilgrim's staff, eating, sleeping, walking, praying with others, and has now returned to complete his work for his degree in counseling those who have been grief stricken.

My other friend, one of the current lay missioners, born with cerebral palsy, using arm crutches to support her weakened limbs, teaches in an alternative high school, teaching our Chicago dropouts. She teaches them far more than English as she traverses three and four flights of stairs, never failing to arrive to educate these disheartened young people on whom the system has given up.

These are but two examples. There are many more.

We have worked in your kitchens and in your classrooms. We have worked in your religious-education classes and in your adult-education programs. Some have been readers and lectors, some have been greeters, and now we seek to do more as full members of the Church, our Church.

What are the physical barriers that keep visually impaired persons, for example, isolated from the local religious community? What keeps us standing outside its open door?

First, print presents a formidable obstacle. Second, we live in a visually oriented society—what you see is all that is important. Our culture lays huge stress on the importance of eye contact. We are cut off from immediate access to *The New World, The National Catholic Reporter,* Sunday bulletins, religious pamphlets, handouts, song sheets, hymnals, signs, and so on.

These are only minor obstacles that can easily be surmounted if the will is there, walls that can easily be broken down with just a little information and research about places and people who put print materials into braille, large print, and cassette, as well as people who will volunteer reading services. We have lots of information to give. Just ask us.

For example, the Xavier Society for the Blind in New York provides the Scriptures, Sunday missals, spiritual materials, and several journals in large print, in braille, and on cassettes, free of charge. They have a toll-free number that perhaps should be in the parish bulletin. They are not the only ones. Many other, local organizations are available, most on a volunteer basis, specifically to bring the world of print into our realm and to free us from isolation. These and local volunteer readers might be listed in the bulletin, or there might even be a hot line to the rectory or some other appropriate location where a blind person might phone and ask for a reader, either one-on-one or over the phone.

The secular world provides this kind of service, and there are already volunteer reading services at several libraries throughout the city.

But these are all superficial constraints—skimming the surface. You must, like Saint-Exupéry's little prince, realize that it is the invisible that is essential. It is what lies beneath, beyond, that is of the essence.

Persons with disabilities are symbols in a true sense, pointing beyond what we are to something that may provide profound insight to God's love. Some cultures believe that the blind are deeply perceptive, have profound insight into all sorts of things. Other cultures—the Middle Eastern, for example—believe that because we cannot see we are less than human, have no souls, are like animals, dogs.

In reality, we are neither, as a rule, but simply people like you, and like you, we wish to become truly integrated members of the community, hoping to share that banquet of which the prophet Isaiah spoke, where all are welcomed to partake of the sweet wines and rich foods, as children of God.

Finally, we are, in truth, a paradox. Acceptance of us into the parish community would seem so simple—the cost is low because there are no architectural barriers, no ramps, no re-designed washrooms that individuals like me need—but the real price is very high. In T. S. Eliot's words, "It is a simple thing, requiring nothing less than everything." Or a metanoia, a complete change of attitude.

Only then will we be able to join you at the banquet table. We are hungry and look forward to such a day. Then we will have a real option for *all* of the poor, or a preferential option for the disabled.

So what is the meaning of this profusion of words, to which we ourselves have now added? Meister Eckhart said, "What good is it to me if Mary gave birth to the son of God fourteen hundred years ago and I do not also give birth to the son of God in my time and in my culture? We are all meant to be Mothers of God."

Will this happen now? Should we all rise up and proclaim the existence of the kingdom in our midst? Hardly. The words I have added to this quest to determine the place of persons with disabilities in the Church are empty unless given sub-stance, enfleshed with action, with real tasks and jobs.

I recall a poem by Emily Dickinson:

> I had been hungry, all the Years—
> My noon had Come—to dine—
> I trembling drew the Table near—
> And touched the Curious Wine—

'Twas this on Tables I had seen—
When turning, hungry, Home
I looked in Windows, for the Wealth
I could not hope—for Mine—

I did not know the ample Bread—
'Twas so unlike the Crumb—
The Birds and I, had often shared
In Nature's—Dining Room—

The Plenty hurt me,—'twas so new—
Myself felt ill—and odd—
As Berry—of a Mountain Bush—
Transplanted—to the Road—

Nor was I hungry—so I found—
That Hunger—was a way
Of Persons outside windows—
The Entering—takes away—

The task is not easy, and our efforts are an ongoing decla-
ration of our real faith in God and what God can bring to the
earth if we choose to allow it to happen. "How shall this be
done?" the disciples asked, and Jesus answered, "With human beings, it is impossible, but with God, all things are possible" (Matthew 19:25–26; author's paraphrase).

We realize that all good things come by grace, that grace
exists only if we work at it, work for it, and work with it, and
that this is never easy.

Appendix

FROM THE VIEWPOINT
OF THE READER

Often, friends or associates, when at ease with a person with a disability, will bring up questions and impressions they have harbored for a long time. Perhaps I can respond to some of the ones that I have heard and thereby open a path to smoother communication and understanding.

Q. Is it proper to ask someone who is handicapped or disabled how they got that way?

A. When? Why? Certainly, to walk up to a perfect stranger in the street and abruptly ask such a question would, obviously, be rude and in very poor taste. This, unfortunately, is often done, and it is difficult for the one under interrogation to maintain a courteous demeanor.

Q. What about asking a question like that when you get to know someone a little better?

A. That's OK, but how much better? In normal intercourse, friends exchange information without any hesitation or embarrassment. If you are really curious, it is better to ask than to burn, but be diplomatic about your curiosity. In other words, would you ask anybody else, friend or casual passerby, such a personal question, or is this liberty reserved for someone with a disability?

Q. What about using certain words? In other words, a matter of appropriate language.

A. I suspect you are wondering if it is OK to use verbs referring to sight or mobility or hearing when speaking with someone who has a particular disability. This is not really an issue at all. People who are in any way challenged use such language among themselves without any problem. People who are blind or visually impaired always refer to "seeing" something or "looking at" something as they touch an object or refer to something they are describing. People who are deaf refer to "hearing" what you said to them, and people who use wheelchairs or walkers refer to walking without any hesitation. It would be far more embarrassing, and even clumsy, to use special words in communicating with someone with a disability than to use everyday terms.

To add another point to the question of language, we are far more sensitive today to inclusive language since feminists have strongly underscored the hidden discrimination in most of our written and verbal literature. That is a question not precisely under consideration.

Further, this question of correct language should also be extended to cultural, racial, and gender rules for courtesy.

If people object to such circumlocution, it is probably because they are speaking from the current vantage point and do not wish to be troubled by thinking before speaking.

An example is always helpful: a relative of mine, wishing that her children would not use negative racial terms, unfortunately taught them to refer to African Americans as "chocolate-faced people."

Q. Is it appropriate to compliment someone by telling them you forgot that they are disabled?

A. People think that this is a compliment and mean it as such; however, it is really a cover-up and actually means just the opposite. What is implied is that you wish the individual were just like you and that you would find that perfectly acceptable. Remember that song from *My Fair Lady* that asks, "Why can't a woman be just like a man?"

What is actually being said is that you cannot accept them as they are but you must think of them without their particular disability.

Q. Is it appropriate to help someone without asking if they want or need your help?

A. This is a very good question. The best thing is to ask someone, friend or stranger, if and what sort of assistance they need, and then follow his or her request for assistance. Do not seize them by the arm, or grasp a guide dog's harness, or try to push an individual's wheelchair. Ask what they need and follow it from there.

Let me share an anecdote about this very dilemma:

My husband, who is very much at east with individuals with a variety of disabilities, noticed a blind man he knew waiting to cross a very busy street at the peak of the rush hour. He got out of his car, approached the man as he waited at the noisy corner, and shouted to him that he would be glad to help him. The noise prevented clear communication, and my husband, thinking he heard what the man said, escorted him across the busy street. When they got to the bus stop, he asked the blind man what bus he was waiting for.

"Oh," my husband said, perplexed, "that's on the other corner where you were standing." With that, he escorted the blind man back to his original position, and they both laughed as they waited together for the correct city bus.

Q. Is it OK to ask someone how they do certain things, like cooking, phoning, traveling, or dressing? Is that being too curious?

A. Not really. People think such questions all the time. It seems that when you get to know someone a little better, it's all right to ask and get their answer.

Q. How do blind persons, or persons with limited vision, know to whom they are speaking?

A. This is a very good and important question. When you meet someone whose vision is impaired, it is proper and very helpful to simply mention your name and then immediately go on with your question or request. It is like a verbal tag that orients the person.

Think of it like answering a phone by mentioning who you are, since you know the person to whom you speak is not yet aware of your identity.

Some voices are unique, but it is not for you to know if yours is or not.

It is also very helpful for you to mention who is in a room when a blind person or someone with limited vision comes in. It is very poor manners to allow someone to think they are alone in the room without offering this courteous bit of information. How would you like to be in such a situation?

WORDS OF INCLUSION

The National Catholic Office for Persons with Disabilities, P.O. Box 29113, Washington, D.C. 20017-0113; 202-529-2933 (v/TTY)

CALLING ON THE CHURCH
TO WELCOME THOSE WITH DISABILITIES

The National Catholic Office for Persons with Disabilities [NCPD] was established in 1982 to foster and promote the challenges issued in the 1978 *U.S. Bishops' Pastoral Statement on Persons with Disabilities*. That landmark document, with its far-ranging vision, inspires and forms the base upon which all activities and programs of NCPD are built. The insights offered by our bishops are as relevant today as they were 15 years ago and form an essential call to action. We must consider the needs, as well as the gifts of over eight million Catholics who live day to day with those disabilities protected under current federal law. Each of these individuals is a mother or father; sister or brother; son or daughter; husband or wife; neighbor or colleague who is essential if the Church is to be truly inclusive. For we are one flock that serves a single Shepherd.

This document is a significant reference for all Catholics who care about justice and dignity for all. The following paragraphs are offered as examples of its inclusive language:

> For most Catholics, the community of believers is embodied in the local parish. The parish is the door to participation for persons with disabilities, and it is the responsibility of the pastor and lay leaders to make sure that this door is always open….In order to be loyal to its calling to be truly pastoral, the parish must make sure that it does not exclude any Catholic who wishes to take part in its activities (paragraph 18).

> Full participation in the Christian community has another important aspect that must not be overlooked. When we think of persons with disabilities in relation to ministry, we tend automatically to think of doing something for them. We do not reflect that they can do something for us and with us….Persons with disabilities can…teach the able-bodied much about strength and Christian acceptance. Moreover, they have the same duty as all members of the community to do the Lord's work in the world, according to their God-given talents and capacities. (paragraph 17).

MESSAGE OF INCLUSION
FROM THE HOLY FATHER

His Holiness Pope John Paul II, You Are the Body of Christ: People with Disability in Society, *delivered November 21, 1992 at the VII Annual Conference of Pontifical Council for Pastoral Assistance to Health Care Workers*

In greetings to 9,000 representatives from 99 countries, His Holiness Pope John Paul II reminded the faithful:

> The words of the topic of this International Conference, *Your Members Are the Body of Christ,* are not a rhetorical expression, but a specific revealed truth from which a clear program for life is deduced….Handicaps, all forms of handi-

caps, never undermine the dignity of the person or the right
to the best quality of life....

In speaking of the rights of people with disabilities, the Holy
Father quoted Pope John XXIII's encyclical *Pacem in Terris:*
"Every human person, as international legislation clearly rec-
ognizes, is the subject of fundamental rights which are inalienable, inviolable, and indivisible." Such an understanding
demands a response on the part of society: "It is necessary to
act in such a way that people with disabilities can feel welcomed into the civil community by full right, being afforded
the effective opportunity to play an active role in the family,
society and the Church. Discretionary assistance, then, en-
trusted to the generosity of some, is not enough: it is necessary for responsible involvement at different levels by all members of the community."

Letter to All U.S. Senators in Support of the Americans with Disabilities Act

Reverend Robert N. Lynch, General Secretary, NCCB/USCC,
September 6, 1989

The U.S. Catholic Conference, the public policy agency of
the nation's Roman Catholic Bishops, offers its general support for the Americans with Disabilities Act....More than ten
years ago in their Pastoral Statement...the bishops called on
Americans to protect the rights of persons with handicaps:

> Defense of the right to life implies the defense of other rights
> which enable the handicapped individual to achieve the
> fullest measure of personal development of which he or she
> is capable. These include the right to equal opportunity in
> education, in employment, in housing, as well as the right
> to free access to public accommodations, facilities and ser-
> vices (paragraph 10).

The Americans with Disabilities Act puts the weight of the federal government in support of these rights of persons with handicapping conditions. Passage of the bill will mean that discrimination solely on the basis of handicaps will be not only immoral, but illegal.

LETTER TO ALL U.S. CATHOLIC BISHOPS

Most Reverend James Malone, Bishop of Youngstown, Ohio, and Chairman, Domestic Policy Committee, USCC, October 24, 1990

The Bishops' conference offered active support for the Americans with Disabilities Act as it passed the Congress and was signed by President Bush. We welcome the new law as a strong and necessary step to end unjust discrimination and to eliminate barriers that unfairly limit the opportunities of persons with disabilities.

Our active support...was based on the clear position adopted by the Conference [in the 1978 *U.S. Bishops' Pastoral Statement on Persons with Disabilities*]:

> Society's frequent indifference of the plight of citizens with disabilities is a problem that cries aloud for solutions based on justice and conscience....All people have a clear duty to do what lies in their power to improve living conditions for persons with disabilities, rather than ignoring them... (paragraph 9). It is not enough merely to affirm the rights of persons with disabilities. We must actively work to realize these rights in the fabric of modern society (paragraph 11).

For solid constitutional reasons, the law does not seek to regulate the conduct of religious bodies....This does not mean or suggest, however, that our strong and continuing support for the full inclusion of our sisters and brothers who have disabling conditions is lessened or limited. We oppose unfair discrimination not because it may be illegal, but because it is wrong. It diminishes both persons with disabilities and the entire Catholic community.

Ten years before the Congress enacted this law, the bishops declared:

> Just as the Church must do all in its power to help ensure persons with disabilities a secure place in the human community, so it must reach out to welcome gratefully those who seek to participate in the ecclesial community... (paragraph 12). If persons with disabilities are to become equal partners in the Christian community, injustices must be eliminated and ignorance and apathy replaced by increased sensitivity and warm acceptance (paragraph 13).

The Catholic Church is working every day to make buildings, programs and ministry of every kind more available to persons with disabilities. This urgent challenge continues, not only for the institutional Church, but for all Catholics....The passage of the Americans with Disabilities Act reminds all of us of our continuing obligation to work for the full participation of people with disabilities in our faith community and the broader society.

We supported this necessary new law, not simply because of what it would do for persons with disabilities...but because of what it could mean for our entire society. We believe our Church and nation will be greatly enriched and strengthened by the broader participation of persons with disabilities under the protections afforded by the Americans with Disabilities Act.

Now is an appropriate time to renew our long-term commitment to accessibility, openness and welcome for all the People of God.

Address to National Conference of Catholic Bishops on the Tenth Anniversary of the Establishment of the National Catholic Office for Persons with Disabilities

Most Reverend Francis E. George, O.M.I., Bishop of Yakima, Washington, and Member of NCPD Board of Directors, November 19, 1992

NCPD has used the 1978 *Pastoral Statement on Persons with Disabilities* as a foundation from which to press for civil legislation which opens previously closed doors in the general society, thereby fostering greater participation in public life on the part of citizens with disabilities. The greatest success in this venture has been the 1990 landmark Americans with Disabilities Act. This act makes it illegal to discriminate in employment, in public services and accommodations, in transportation and telecommunications against anyone who has a mental or physical disability. More positively, this law sets out patterns and means for helping people with disabilities become functional in situations which previously handicapped them.

All of us...can take satisfaction in this movement toward making ours a more participatory Church and civil society....In the Church, there is much greater access by the disabled to the sacraments and to various ministries. There is much greater awareness of how many people with disabilities there really are in our parishes and dioceses. There have been significant changes in attitudes towards our sisters and brothers with disabilities.

Grateful for this, the Board of NCPD hopes that the U.S. Church's self-understanding will continue to grow to appreciate the gift and the power of vulnerability, made visible in the disabled among us. Vulnerability creates relationships. It helps to create the interdependence which contributes to ecclesial communion. It reverses the false ideal of total personal independence. NCPD hopes that more and more, the Church will see herself as a community of solidarity with the vulnerable. In shifting the paradigm of inclusivity from disability to vulnerability, we come to see how the disabled have a particular gift to contribute precisely because they are limited.

In society, there has also been a shift in recent years from a medical model, which sees those physically or mentally impaired, to a political model, which conceptualizes the environment as the handicapping factor. The disabled have now been identified as a minority group whose individual rights have to be protected in law. This movement or shift is understandable, given the fact that the language of individual rights is the only public discourse available to us in the United States. This shift, however, easily reinforces the notion that, finally, we are what we can do and that the ability to participate, to be related to the community depends upon some ability to function. While this presupposition moves us to include people by making them as functional as possible, it can also serve to excuse our excluding those who, despite all our efforts, and all technological advances, are unable to function effectively. The test case remains those so severely disabled that they are almost totally dependent on others, those who cannot now and will never be particularly skilled or able to speak or function effectively. Faith tells us they are valuable not because of what they can do but because they are loved by an infinite God.

Words from NCPD's Executive Director

Mary Jane Owen, You Are the Body of Christ: People with Disability in Society, *delivered at the VII Annual Conference of Pontifical Council for Pastoral Assistance to Health Care Workers, November 20, 1992*

In addressing this conference on *The Wisdom of Human Vulnerability: Disability—The Tie Which Binds,* NCPD Executive Director Mary Jane Owen noted:

> There is wisdom and uniting power in the vulnerability of the human body but we may need to alter the conceptual lenses through which we have traditionally viewed assorted disabilities.
>
> Current medical and rehabilitation technology and techniques can assist our brothers and sisters; sons and daughters; husbands and wives; mothers and fathers to remain interactive and involved with those whom they love and who love them as various functions diminish or are lost. I do not propose an end to our efforts to reduce suffering, only that we approach those challenges with deepened awareness that vulnerability may be an essential component in God's plan for us.
>
> The judgment "I'd rather be dead than disabled" is a painful reminder of the low value placed upon our lives. And this troublesome refrain collides with our views about the sanctity of life. For it fuels those outmoded fears about unwanted dependency which are associated with "infirmities" and moves people to choose death over inconvenient life. Whether a given eugenics campaign endorses euthanasia, infanticide or amniocentesis and abortion, potential colleagues are easy prey to each retelling of the ancient and no longer appropriate terror. The assaults upon life move forward because so few of us are knowledgeable or comfortable enough to speak out positively about the power of the powerless and the potential of those who are disabled.
>
> And the pious reinforce this negativity as they mutter, "There but for the grace of God go I," failing to recognize the verdict they have leveled against those who live with disabilities and who may still be well within the circle of God's grace and love.

Against this sketchy background, let us quickly examine a few conceptual lenses which will allow us to glimpse the potential of those with disabilities:

1. A shifting paradigm replaces the medical model, which sees those with impairments as "patients" whose needs must be met in "special" ways with a political socio-economic alternative which conceptualizes the environment as the handicapping factor.
2. A new definition asserts: "Disabilities" are the normal and anticipated outcome of the risks, strains and stresses of the living process itself. Therefore, the condition ceases to be merely an individual tragedy and becomes an expectation within any community.
3. The symbol of the Cross is essential to our Faith, but we are the Easter people who look beyond Calvary to the sunrise of that glorious dawn when the heavy stone blocking our view of His power and grace is rolled away. The old association of disabilities with the suffering Christ can be expanded to include the miracles of rehabilitation as small reminders of His Resurrection. Thus we confirm we are a part of His Body and our souls strive to prove His power.
4. Each time words of pity target those with disabilities the message of inclusion is blunted. Pity limits, shames and never elevates the one toward whom it is directed. It is an unwanted projection of society's fear and discomfort. Respectful compassion and mutual recognition of our shared fragility must replace it if we are to become united as people of God.
5. The fifth lens is pivotal if we are to justify the challenge of this new orientation, for a new prescription calls for a lens which can focus on the power of human vulnerability. Until we recognize this trait as valuable to the health of any organization, we will lack motivation to alter our current patterns of exclusion and separateness.

OUR VULNERABILITY, WHICH HAS BEEN ENCODED INTO OUR GENE POOL, IS THE CATALYST WHICH BRINGS US INTO COMMUNITY AND CHURCH WITH RENEWED RECOGNITION THAT WE NEED EACH

OTHER AND OUR LORD. When God tied the gift of life to the trait of vulnerability, God may have given us the only incentive which could counter our tendency toward disregard of the rights and value of others. When we see ourselves in our peers, we are joined in a bond which comes from the heart. When we are unaware of or deny our interconnectedness, we move about functioning as if our souls had been placed in high impact plastic bodies. We tend to become alienated and solitary, mistaking independence as the source of power. We take a "Kleenex" approach toward life, justifying its disposal when it becomes less than perfect.

It is through synergy and mutual aid that communities are built and maintained. Without the evidence of our own weakness and fragility, many of us would ignore the message of unity and interaction. When Christ called upon us to seek the safety of the fold, the message was of our need, not our ability to thrive in isolation.

Too many individuals with disabilities have awaited their turn to worship and to serve their Lord. Too often the Good News has been proclaimed behind barriers we could not overcome and our potential contributions have gone unnoticed. Upon signing the Americans with Disabilities Act, our President told the thousands assembled on the White House lawn that this law was a sledgehammer with which to smash the ancient walls which had blocked 43 million people from fulfilling their dreams and offering their gifts to the nation. That wall of prejudice and fear extends around the globe, separating and segregating.

A united resolve to smash the old conceptual lenses which blurred our vision of the power of human vulnerability can destroy the old prejudices. We must constantly remind ourselves that God's gift of life is placed in fragile earthen vessels to a powerful purpose. We have only to recognize and celebrate that reality and it will free us from past fears.

For it is our common recognition of interdependency which weaves the threads of our societies together. Each time one of us feels needed and essential to another, the threads of that interaction are reinforced and the fabric which holds us together as Church and as society is powerfully strengthened.

There is wisdom in vulnerability and it will bind us together powerfully, if we will only look at the reality with fresh vision.

May God bless our crusade.

Reprinted with permission from Opening Doors to People with Disabilities, *Vol. 1, National Catholic Office for Persons with Disabilities, Washington, D.C., 1995, 137-64.*

AMERICANS WITH DISABILITIES ACT FACT SHEET

Distributed by the National Catholic Office for Persons with Disabilities, P.O. Box 29113, Washington, D.C. 20017-0113; 202-529-2933 (v/TTY); Executive Director: Mary Jane Owen

WITH SPECIFIC REFERENCES TO RELIGIOUS INSTITUTIONS INCLUDED

Employers

- May not discriminate against an individual with a disability in hiring or promotion if the person is otherwise qualified for the job.
- Can ask about one's ability to perform a job, but cannot inquire if someone has a disability or subject a person to tests that tend to screen out people with disabilities.
- Will need to provide "reasonable accommodation" to individuals with disabilities. This includes steps such as job restructuring and modification of equipment.

- Do not need to provide accommodations that impose an "undue hardship" on business operations.
- With 25 or more employees must comply, effective July 26, 1992.
- With 15–24 employees must comply, effective July 26, 1994.

> A religious corporation, association, educational institution, or society may give a preference in employment to individuals of the particular religion, and may require that applicants and employees conform to the religious tenets of the organization. However, a religious organization may not discriminate against an individual who satisfies the permitted religious criteria because that individual is disabled. The religious entity, in other words, is required to consider qualified individuals with disabilities who satisfy the permitted religious criteria on an equal basis with qualified individuals without disabilities who similarly satisfy the religious criteria (United States Employment Opportunity Commission Final ADA Rule, July, 1991).

Transportation

- New public transit buses ordered after August 26, 1990, must be accessible to individuals with disabilities.
- Transit authorities must provide comparable paratransit or other special transportation services to individuals with disabilities who cannot use fixed route bus service, unless an undue burden would result.
- Existing rail systems must have one accessible car per train by July 26, 1995.
- New rail cars ordered after August 26, 1990, must be accessible.
- New bus and train stations must be accessible.
- Key stations in rapid, light, and commuter rail systems must be made accessible by July 26, 1993, with extensions up to 20 years for commuter rail (30 years for rapid and light rail).
- All existing Amtrak stations must be accessible by July 26, 2010.

State and Local Governments

- State and local governments may not discriminate against qualified individuals with disabilities.
- All government facilities, services and communications must be accessible consistent with the requirements of Section 504 of the Rehabilitation Act of 1973.

Public Accommodations

- Private entities such as restaurants, hotels, and retail stores may not discriminate against individuals with disabilities, effective January 26, 1992.
- Auxiliary aids and services must be provided to individuals with vision or hearing impairments or other individuals with disabilities, unless an undue burden would result.
- Physical barriers in existing facilities must be removed, if removal is readily achievable. If not, alternative methods of providing the services must be offered, if they are readily achievable.
- All new construction and alterations of facilities must be accessible.

The ADA's exemption of religious organizations and religious entities controlled by religious organizations is very broad, encompassing a wide variety of situations. Religious organizations and entities controlled by religious organizations have no obligations under the public accommodation requirements of ADA. Even when a religious organization carries out activities that would otherwise make it a public accommodation, the religious organization is exempt from ADA coverage. Thus, if a church itself operates a day care center, a nursing home, a private school, or a diocesan school system, the operations of the center, home, school, or schools would not be subject to the requirements of the ADA or this part. The religious entity would not lose its exemption merely because the services provided were open to the general public. The test is whether the church or other religious organization operates the public accommodation, not which individuals receive the public accommodation's services.

Religious entities that are controlled by religious organizations are also exempt from the ADA's requirements. Many religious organizations in the United States use lay boards and other secular or corporate mechanisms to operate schools and an array of social services. The use of a lay board or other mechanism does not itself remove the ADA's religious exemption. Thus, a parochial school, having religious doctrine in its curriculum and sponsored by a religious order, could be exempt either as a religious organization or as an entity controlled by a religious organization, even if it has a lay board. The test remains a factual one—whether the church or other religious organization controls the operations of the school or of the service or whether the school or service is itself a religious organization.

Although a religious organization or a religious entity that is controlled by a religious organization has no obligations under the rule, a public accommodation that is not itself a religious organization, but that operates a place of public accommodation in leased space on the property of a religious entity, which is not a place of worship, is subject to the rule's requirements if it is not under control of a religious organization. When a church rents meeting space, which is not a place of worship, to a local community group or to a private, independent day care center, the ADA applies to the activities of the local community group and day care center if a lease exists and consideration is paid (United States Department of Justice Final ADA Rule, July, 1991).

Telecommunications

- Companies offering telephone service to the general public must offer telephone relay services to individuals who use telecommunications devices for the deaf (TDDs) or similar devices, effective July 26, 1993.

Reprinted with permission from ADA Awareness Packet, *National Catholic Office for Persons with Disabilities, Washington, D.C., 1993.*

COURTESY RULES
UPON MEETING
A DISABLED PERSON

Often, when meeting a person with an obvious disability, awkwardness may be avoided if certain basic rules of courtesy are followed:

1. Assume that the individual is an adult and capable of ordinary means of communication; that is, don't raise your voice or address the person as you might speak to a child. Don't inquire of others what the person might want— cream in the coffee, or location of the bathroom. Speak to the person, and he or she will respond.

2. If a person with any obvious disability is walking with you, do not take his or her arm or seize hold of the wheelchair or whatever device he or she is using, and do not take hold of a guide dog's harness. Let the disabled person take your arm or let you know what is needed. Simply ask if your help is needed.

3. It is good to let someone who cannot see know who is in

the room when he or she enters, and to introduce the person with a disability to the others in the room, including the children. To help a blind person to a seat, simply place his or her hand on the back of a chair, to orient him or her to its direction.

4. The door to a room, cabinet, or car left partially open is a hazard, especially to someone who is very tall or who cannot see it.

5. At dinner or breakfast it would be good to inform someone who cannot see what is on the table or what is being served. In the case of someone who has another physical limitation, ask how you may be of assistance.

6. Don't avoid words like "see" or "walk" because persons with disabilities use these words as readily as anyone else.

7. Persons with disabilities do not want pity or patronizing praise. Do not assume that because someone has a limitation, other senses are more acute. That is simply not true. Certainly, if someone must depend on memory more than usual, it simply means memory may be more developed because it is needed.

8. If you have a houseguest with special needs, simply inform him or her of the location of the facilities, and of what is available for use, and assume that will be adequate.

9. If you are curious about someone's disability, you may inquire about this when you are better acquainted. Remember, it's an old story for him or her. Many other interests have occupied his or her life, and it is to these that any person with or without a disability would far more happily turn for mature discussion.

10. The ultimate rule is to realize that each human being is a person with rich potential and special gifts, and it is these that make the individual worth knowing.

In all fifty states, the law requires drivers to yield the right of way when they see a white cane or guide dog or wheel-chair. In fact, more persons with all sorts of limitations are visible in society today because attitudes are changing and opportunities are becoming more available.

SOURCES

ADA Awareness Packet. Washington, D.C.: National Catholic Office for Persons with Disabilities, 1993.

Benton, Janice L. and Mary Jane Owen. *Opening Doors to People with Disabilities* vol. 1. Washington, D.C.: National Catholic Office for Persons with Disabilities, 1995.

Berger, Peter L. *A Rumor of Angels.* New York: Doubleday, 1990.

Browne, Elizabeth J. *God Is Blind: A Liberation Theology of the Outcast* (unpublished master's thesis). Chicago: Catholic Theological Union, 1991.

———. "Samson: Riddle and Paradox." *The Bible Today* (May 1984): 161–67.

———. "Siloam" (poem). *The Bible Today* (May 1987): 187.

Celebrate and Challenge. Washington, D.C.: National Catholic Office for Persons with Disabilities, 1988.

Cone, James H. *A Black Theology of Liberation.* Maryknoll, N.Y.: Orbis, 1986.

Drury, John. *Tradition and Design in Luke's Gospel.* London: Darton, Longman and Todd, 1976.

Eiesland, Nancy L. *The Disabled God: Toward a Liberation Theology of Disability.* Nashville: Abingdon Press, 1994.

Erikson, Erik H. *Dimensions of a New Identity: Jefferson Lectures.* New York: Norton, 1973.

Fiorenza, Elisabeth Schussler. *Bread Not Stone: The Challenge of Feminist Biblical Interpretation.* Boston: Beacon, 1984.

———. *In Memory of Her.* New York: Crossroads, 1984.

Fitzmyer, Joseph A. *Luke the Theologian.* New York: Paulist, 1989.

Foley, Edward, O.S.F., ed. *Developmental Disabilities and Sacramental Access.* Chicago: Archdiocesan Office of Divine Worship, 1994.

Frankl, Viktor E. *Man's Search for Meaning.* New York: Simon and Schuster, 1973.

Fretheim, Terence E. *The Suffering of God: An Old Testament Perspective.* Philadelphia: Fortress, 1946.

Häring, Bernard. *Free and Faithful in Christ.* Vol. 1 of *General Moral Theology for Clergy and Laity.* New York: Seabury, 1978–82.

Hiebert, Paul. "Critical Contextualization." *International Bulletin of Missionary Research* 11 (1987): 104–12.

Ide, Arthur F. and William E. Tanner. *Jews, Jesus and Women in the Apostolic Age.* Mesquite, Tex.: Ide House, 1984.

John XXIII, Pope. *Mater et Magistra.* May 15, 1961.

———. *Gaudium et Spes.* Dec. 7, 1965.

John Paul II, Pope. *Laborem Exercens.* Sept. 14, 1981.

———. *Address to Crippled and Disabled Persons of Work.* Mar. 14, 1981.

———. *The Handicapped in Modern Society.* Sept. 10, 1984.

Johnson, Elizabeth A. "The Incomprehensibility of God and the Image of God, Male and Female." *Theological Studies* 45 (1984): 441–65.

Krafft, Jane, M.S.B.T. *The Ministry to Persons with Disabilities.* Collegeville, Minn.: Liturgical, 1988.

Leo XIII, Pope. *Rerum Novarum.* May 15, 1891.

McFague, Sallie. *Models of God: Theology in an Ecological, Nuclear Age.* Philadelphia: Fortress, 1987.

Maida, Archbishop Adam: "Persons with Disabilities: Attitude, Accommodation and Architecture" (on the fifteenth anniversary of the *Pastoral Statement of U.S. Catholic Bishops on People with Disabilities*). *Origins* (Oct. 28, 1993).

Paul VI, Pope. *Populorum Progressio.* Mar. 26, 1967.

Pius XI, Pope. *Quadragesimo Anno.* May 15, 1931.

Rahner, Karl. *Foundations of Christian Faith.* New York: Crossroads, 1982.

———. "Theology of Freedom." *Theological Investigations.* vol. 1.

Schreiter, Robert. *Constructing Local Theologies.* Maryknoll, N.Y.: Orbis, 1985.

Senior, Donald. *The Passion of Jesus in the Gospel of Luke.* Wilmington, Del.: Glazier, 1989.

Senior, Donald, et al., ed. *The Catholic Study Bible.* New York: Oxford, 1990.

Shapiro, Joseph P. *No Pity: People with Disabilities Forging a New Civil Rights Movement.* New York: Random House, 1993.

Springer, Robert. *Conscience and the Behavioral Sciences.* Washington, D.C.: Corpus Books, 1969.

Trible, Phyllis. *God and the Rhetoric of Sexuality.* Minneapolis: Fortress, 1978.

U.S. Conference of Catholic Bishops. *Pastoral Letter on the Economy.* Washington, D.C.: Nov. 1986.

———. *Celebrate and Challenge: On the Ten Year Anniversary of the Pastoral Statement on People with Disabilities.* Washington, D.C.: 1988.

———. *Pastoral Statement of U.S. Catholic Bishops on Persons with Disabilities.* Washington, D.C.: Nov. 16, 1978.

———. *Guidelines for the Celebration of the Sacraments with Persons with Disabilities.* Washington, D.C.: 1995.

U.S. Department of Education, Office for Civil Rights. *The Rights of Individuals with Handicaps under Federal Law.* Washington, D.C.: U.S. Government Printing Office, 1992.
———. *Notice of Nondiscrimination.* Washington, D.C.: U.S. Government Printing Office, Apr. 1991.

ADDITIONAL RESOURCES

For additional information about ministry to and with people with disabilities, the reader may write to or telephone the following:

1. National Catholic Office for Persons with Disabilities
   Mary Jane Owen, Executive Director
   P.O. Box 29113
   Washington, D.C. 20017-0113
   Tel: (202) 529-2933 (v/TTY)
   NCPD publishes a newsletter as well as books, pamphlets, and videotapes providing information on the inclusion of persons with all types of disabilities in Catholic churches in the United States. NCPD is considered the national voice of the National Conference of Catholic Bishops with respect to the bishops' concerns for the 10 million U.S. Catholics with disabilities.

2. National Catholic Office for the Deaf
   7202 Buchanan Street
   Landover, MD 20984

Tel: (301) 577-1684
TTY: (301) 577-4184
This office provides information to and about persons with hearing problems and will provide local information to agencies and organizations working exclusively with persons with hearing problems.

3. Xavier Society for the Blind and Physically Disabled
   Rev. Alfred Caruana, S.J., Director
   154 East 23rd Street
   New York, NY 10010
   Tel: (800) 637-9193
   The Xavier Society provides religious materials in three formats—braille, large print, and cassettes—to persons with visual and reading disabilities. The society also provides several versions of the Bible, a newsletter, Catholic publications, and books, free of charge to eligible members.

4. National Council for Independent Living
   2111 Wilson Boulevard, Suite 405
   Arlington, VA 22201
   Tel: (703) 525-3406
   This office provides information about local facilities and organizations working for independent living conditions for persons with physical disabilities.

5. National Council on Disabilities
   1331 F Street NW, Suite 1050
   Washington, D.C. 20004
   Tel: (202) 272-2004
   This office provides information to persons with a variety of disabilities—purely on a secular level—and should be a source to direct persons to appropriate local organizations.

INDEX

ABOUT THE AUTHOR

E lizabeth (Prete) Browne is an associate lector at Mundelein College of Loyola University in Chicago. She has a
doctoral degree in English and a master's degree in philosophy, both from Loyola. In 1991 she was the first blind person
to receive a master of theological studies (MTS) degree from
Catholic Theological Union, the culmination of her lifelong
interest in religious matters.

She has taught in several Chicago-area universities and col-
leges as well as in the archdiocesan college seminary.

She is married to Edward Browne, has five children, and
has always been actively involved in work on behalf of persons with disabilities, as well as in religious- and civil-rights
efforts. She serves on the board of Blind Service Association
in Chicago and is an active member of the National Federa-
tion of the Blind.